Praise for COLTER

"A luminous book about a relationship . . . Bass is a masterly writer, driven by the same passion that makes Colter hunt down pheasants until his face is soaked with snow-white slobber." — *USA Today*

"Exhilarating . . . perfectly pitched . . . *Colter* tells the truth as unerringly as a good dog gone on point." — **David Gutterson**

"[A] gorgeous, heart-tugging man-and-dog memoir . . . Bass, one of our living masters, shows a flawless touch with tone and emotional rhythm, shifting from comedy to elegy with spellbinding ease, and the book's every page has some image or idea that illuminates the heart of life." — *Milwaukee Journal Sentinel*

"The most impressive work for Bass in years . . . as clean and clear as the human and natural landscape it explores." — *Boston Globe*

"What hard-core dog lover doesn't see his or her dog through that soft-focus lens of love? . . . Bass's book inhabits a world of golden autumnal light that illuminates this love perfectly."
— *Washington Post*

"Bass's writing style is crystalline, see-through to the bottom, a purity of style well matched to the task of capturing Colter's purity of living . . . He writes about such un-postmodern concepts as grace, gratitude, love, and loss with refreshing honesty . . . Although the end of this tale is a sad one, readers can't help but be grateful that we too were allowed to share in Colter's exuberance."
— *Denver Rocky Mountain News*

"Rick Bass writes on something of a superhuman plane in *Colter;* he was mad in love with his dog . . . and that's what you read these pages for: To be in the presence of an intense man completely given over to passion. And who can write breathtakingly about it . . . If any writer can awaken a taste for the outdoors, Bass can."
— *Detroit Free Press*

"Colter is a dog of boundless spirit, all grace and wild genius. And his terrific master, Rick Bass, happens to be a national treasure. What a terrific team they make!" — **Carl Hiaasen**

"Bass brings skill to his passionate portrait of his late German short-haired pointer." — *Chicago Tribune*

COLTER

The True Story
of the
Best Dog I Ever Had

Rick Bass

A Mariner Book
HOUGHTON MIFFLIN COMPANY
BOSTON · NEW YORK

First Mariner Books edition 2001

Visit our Web site: www.houghtonmifflinbooks.com.

Library of Congress Cataloging-in-Publication Data
Bass, Rick, date.
Colter : the true story of the best dog I ever
had / Rick Bass.
p.   cm.
ISBN 0-395-92618-1
ISBN 0-618-12736-4 (pbk.)
1. Hunting dogs — Montana — Yaak Valley — Anecdotes.
2. Dog owners — Montana — Yaak Valley — Anecdotes.
3. Human-animal relationships — Montana — Yaak Valley
— Anecdotes. 4. Bass, Rick, 1958–. I. Title.
SF428.5 .B336 2000
636.752'09786'81 — dc21   00-020524

Printed in the United States of America

Book design by Robert Overholtzer

QUM 10 9 8 7 6 5 4 3 2 1

*For John Graves and wild birds,
and for Elizabeth,
Mary, Katherine, and Lowry*

Prologue

I'D SEE my friend Tom walking up and down the roads, dressed in buckskin made from the deer hide he and his wife, Nancy, had tanned, with a hawk on one arm and a beautiful brown dog, whose name I learned later was Paggon, running along in front of him. I knew Tom was hunting grouse, and I'd wave and drive on, never imagining the changes that were soon to come. The aspen and cottonwood trees were stripped bare, as were the limbs of the alder, and smoke was rising from the chimneys of the cabins along the river as the valley tucked itself in for winter.

Paggon's pups were born in May. I never saw the litter. I didn't know Tom and Nancy had been selling them, one by one, through May and June.

That June I was out in my little shed, writing, when I heard a truck pull in the drive. It was Nancy, seemingly aswarm with dogs: three brown heads like dolls in the front seat with her — Paggon and two gangly pups swarming her, licking her. As I stepped out of the shed Paggon leapt out, the pups tumbling out after her — one stocky and bullish, the other bony, cross-legged, pointy-headed, goofy-looking. The goofy one ran toward me, barking and growling and leaping up at me. I put my arms out and caught him. Nancy told me Paggon had had a litter in May, and the one I was holding was the last one left; the stocky one, Bridger, being already spoken for. She claimed she had come by only to borrow a cup of sugar, but before she left I had written her a check for that last pup, the runt of the litter, the one nobody else wanted. Something about the goofy little knot-headed dog made me laugh.

How we fall into grace. You can't work or earn your way into it. You just fall. It lies below, it lies beyond. It comes to you, unbidden.

The first photograph I have of Colter shows our then two-year-old, Mary Katherine, burying him in aspen leaves, piling handful after handful of them on him while he lies there patiently, with gold leaves like coins against his rich deep brown coat.

My hunting partner, Tim, had a reserved and elegant, even queenly, golden retriever, Maddie. She came from pet lines, not hunting lines, but he had trained her to hunt simply by having such good communication with her, by showing her, explaining to her in that unspoken language of dog and man, what he wanted her to do. Sculpting her with his passion: shaping and

bending her through yes's and no's, smiles and repri-
mands, laughs and smiles. It was an amazing thing to
see. Her job as a flushing dog was to gallop through
the woods, find the spooky grouse, and pursue them
until their only chance was to leap into the air and try
to fly away fast. At which time Tim had one, maybe
two, seconds to take a shot.

Colter's role was the opposite of Maddie's. His breeding, his blood — the earth and history — called for him
not to flush the birds, but to set up on point as close as
he could get to a bird without frightening it.

Every bird-dog trainer in the world will tell you not
to run a pointing dog and a flushing dog together. The
pointing dog will begin to enjoy flushing the birds, and
the flushing dog might begin to lose its natural ability
to get the bird into the air at close distance to the
hunter.

And maybe they're right. Maybe this was the one
time, the only time, in the history of dogs that it ever
worked. But these two dogs, an old female and a
young male, were just friendly enough and competitive
enough to challenge each other to perform at a higher
level — as if each, in a kind of stubbornness, sought to
convert the other to his or her way of being-in-the-
world through the force of luminous example.

It might have been a cardinal sin, but damn it was
fun. Occasionally they would look back over their
shoulders at each other, and sometimes at us, but usually they were pushing wildly forward, surging, always
forward; and the world, the fields around us, crackled,
doubly rich with two kinds of energy, those two styles
of hunting at once.

It revved the dogs up, as well as us. The word *addiction* has such a negative ring to it; I suppose I should say that we were *more fully engaged* when hunting with them; *more intimately connected to the natural world*. But an addiction is what it was.

They moved through the dense woods of this dark valley and across the gold prairies of the east side, so fast that you could have sworn the color of electricity was not blue or silver, but instead brown, Colter, and gold, Maddie.

We didn't know what we were doing: only that we couldn't do without it.

Colter was born wild, born ready. In that sense he was irreducible. All the rest of his training would involve a paring-down from that initial and innate fullness, rather than a building-up. Out of such gradual reduction, his force, his excellence, was magnified.

There was, however, no whittling down, that first year. Tim and I, not knowing any better, just laughed, and let him run wilder, bigger, following the siren odors of scent into the next county, or the next state — which, with his incredible nose, he could miraculously detect.

On our first trip across the Continental Divide, over to the east side of Montana, to hunt pheasants, Tim and I were curious as to how the dogs would react to a species they had never hunted before. The pheasants tended to run great distances, we knew, at high speeds, so that neither would they flush for a flushing dog nor hold tight for a pointing dog.

It was early December, wicked-cold and windy. We drove the six hard hours through the snowy mountains and came out onto the plains with still about an hour of light left in the day. The Rocky Mountains, majestic beneath the day's new snow, loomed behind us now. It was strange and beautiful, looking at them from a slight distance — from the other side — rather than being immersed deep within them.

We knocked on a farmer's door; got permission to hunt, got directions. We drove to the field and put on our gear, loaded our guns, and stepped out into the north wind: its forty-mile-per-hour gusts.

The dogs never looked back. They leapt from the back of the truck and ran barking to the north, running neck and neck, faster than I would have believed dogs could run, straight into the headwind.

From time to time they would make the faintest, slightest adjustment in their beeline, as if the pheasant they were running had altered its course left or right by a foot or two — but for the most part it was as if they were following a line straight as railroad tracks, and they ran north into the blue dusk and over the horizon, barking joyously. In two minutes they were a mile distant; in five minutes, we could not see them. Tim and I hiked north into the bitter wind — we'd forgotten to bring gloves, so we unloaded our guns and walked with our hands tucked under our armpits, arms crossed, as if imitating the winged walk of some awkward birds — and we talked and shivered. The dogs returned to us shortly after dark, and that was our first pheasant hunt. *Nothing.*

There was to be only one really perfect point that season, that whole year. It was back in our valley, right before dark, and Tim and I were driving home from an afternoon's hunt, birdless again. Tim spotted a lone mature ruffed grouse back in the woods — giant larch trees all around — and we stopped and turned out Colter to see what he would do. I stepped into the woods and loaded my gun.

Colter picked up the scent where the bird had crossed the road, and then, rather than ground-trailing it to the source, he instinctively lifted his head high and moved straight in to the scent's origin — ignoring, rejecting immediately, the residue, the leavings.

He approached the bird, then slammed on point as if piling into a brick wall. I stepped up and flushed the bird. It flew fast and low between the big trees, a dark blur in dim light. I almost waited too long. I finally poked a shot at it and the bird tumbled. Colter, who was still on point, went on my command to fetch the bird. He brought it all the way in to me, eager in his puppyness to please. (After adolescence — or, as Nancy puts it, "after his beans dropped" — he stopped retrieving birds, as if concentrating only on his business, his breeding — the discovering and pointing of them. His higher calling. The brown dog as artist.)

My friend, the hunter and writer Jim Fergus, has said that he doesn't remember any of his great shots, nor the occasional mistakes his dog makes. It's the exact opposite, he says, and he's right: you remember the great moments of the dog's work — they are scribed in your mind permanently, down to every last detail — and you remember only your missed shots, the ones (and there are hundreds of them) where you let the dog down.

It seems in this regard quite the opposite of all our other human ventures, where we tend to exaggerate our successes and gloss over or minimize our low points. It's like an inversion of our true nature, I think — the opposite of regular life. You could say that it, hunting with a dog, is the opposite of life; that it is a pursuit toward the death of a thing — the birds. But tell me then why it is that it's when I feel most alive — trailing behind Colter, watching him take scent of the world, watching him make game: building toward that thunderous moment when he finds the bird, and the bird gets up, and I shoot, and hit or miss.

I don't like missing. I usually do — I'm used to it — but I don't like it.

Hunting with a dog, you go past a certain place in the world, and in yourself. The best way I can describe it to someone who doesn't hunt is that it's like traveling into new country, new territory: some unexplored land, still in this life, but so sensate and crisp as to seem beyond this life; everything is felt more sharply, more intimately, and at a smoother, more supple pace. Even when things are happening fast in the field there is a slowed down, or timeless, quality. At the end of a day your eyes are dry and red from not blinking, from staring wide-eyed at all the rawness you see and feel each day, hunting, and from not wanting to miss seeing anything.

It is a different feeling when you shoot at a bird and drop it, instead of shooting and missing, even if your and the dog's pursuit, and the dog's execution of his or her talent, is the pinnacle of the day, the high point, the best part.

Hitting a bird is like going still further or deeper into new country. It is like leaving some other place behind. It is an amazing journey back to the place we came from — back to a time when we hunted to stay alive — the place where we spent the first 99.5 percent of our existence as a species.

Maybe it's a sign of the failure of a few of us to evolve. Perhaps this feeling I have, when hunting, of being on a much needed, even spiritual and necessary journey — a deep familiarity and comfort with the world — speaks to a regression, an inability to keep up with modern life. A damnable Paleolithic gene, so that I just can't help myself. All of which may very well be true. People fearful or disapproving of hunting may see it as a turning-away from the human race, and a turning-back.

But it does not feel that way to me. When autumn comes and I go into the field with Colter, I feel more alive than at any of the other time — as if, for the previous nine months I, and the rest of the world, have been sleeping — and that the rest of the world continues sleeping, back in the villages of man, while I, and a few others, awaken, and travel to a luminous new country just beyond the borders of the sleeping town.

It doesn't feel as if I am returning to the past, journeying backward. It never feels like anything less than continuing to move forward, ceaselessly forward, as we have always done: the great crush and mass of history pushing from behind.

I could no more not feel the way I do about hunting than I could stop the turning of the Earth. For me, it was set in motion a long time ago.

I love my life the other nine months of the year — which is what makes it all the more amazing to me that, as wonderful as my life is, come September, it is nonetheless like an awakening, a journeying beyond even that halcyon life.

You can imagine, please, how grateful I am to my dog — to Colter, the brown bomber — for awakening me from this sleeping shell or cyst. For taking me into new territory.

One

AFTER that first miracle season — miraculous if only for one grouse at dusk, in which flame leapt from the end of the gun — I had a hard decision to make. I didn't know much about birds, or bird-hunting, but I knew that I had a raging genius on my hands. And I'd bragged on him to my friend Jarrett Thompson, the best trainer in the world, who was anxious to see Colter and to work with him.

Jarrett's Old South Pointer Farm was in Texas, though, and it seemed inconceivable to me to separate from Colter. To not be the one to feed him twice a day — to not have him bounding ahead of me on walks. To not see him for weeks at a time — as if he had cast too far out in front of me, working some thin ribbon of scent. As if he were up ahead, hunting without me.

I went back and forth in my mind, tortured. It took about a month before I finally decided to do what was best for Colter, rather than for me. I flew to Houston with him in the spring, and then my father and I drove him up to Jarrett's place.

Jarrett complimented Colter on his good looks: he was the only brown dog on the farm, amidst perhaps a hundred other white dogs — white and lemon pointers, white and liver ones. Colter's muscles stood out deeper than those of the other dogs. I said my good-byes to him and left, and I carried with me that huge and strangely empty feeling of having made a life-changing, or life-turning, decision, but having no clue whatsoever whether it was the right one.

Some people say pointers are crazy, others say it is their owners. Jarrett's too diplomatic to take sides, but he has some stories.

One of his favorite's is about this big hunter from Florida — big in the sense that he weighed three hundred pounds. The guy came to Jarrett's farm to drop his dog off, and at the moment of parting, he hugged his dog — a monster itself, an English pointer weighing almost eighty pounds — and then he took Jarrett aside and handed him a gallon of Jack Daniels.

"Now Thompson," he says, "Old Buck and I each have a glass of whiskey in the evenings after we get through hunting, and I expect y'all to do the same."

Then there was the oil man from west Texas, Odessa, who decided he wanted a bird dog — one of the best — but he wanted a friendly dog, one he could keep in the house. So he flew to Rosanky in his Lear jet and picked out one of the dogs Jarrett had raised and trained to sell. It cost him about three thousand dollars to bring the jet over there, and another twenty-five hundred for the dog, Ned. Jarrett drove him back to the airport in Austin, where the jet was waiting, oil derricks painted on its tail. The oil man put Ned right up there in the front seat and strapped him in with the shoulder harness next to the pilot, Ned looking all around and wondering, perhaps, if he would ever hunt again. The pilot, says Thompson, was rolling his eyes — dog hair on the seat and Ned panting, Ned slobbering.

A week later Thompson got a call from the oil man. "I think Ned's homesick," he said. "Can I fly him home and give him back to you? I'll pay you a thousand dollars to take him. All he does is lie around by the refrigerator," the man said. "I think he misses you, and misses the other dogs. I feel bad about it."

Another pointer-owner came driving down the road one day, bringing his dog along, wanting to see what Jarrett's farm was like. He was thinking about leaving his dog, Sarge, in Jarrett's care.

"I had him take me out in the woods," Jarrett says, "just to see what kind of dog Sarge was — what he could do, and what I could expect from him. To see if he had any spark.

"Before we started to do anything, though, the guy — I can't remember his name either — asks if he can have a minute with Sarge, and I say sure, not knowing what's up, and he takes Sarge off a little ways and tells him to *sit*, and then he starts *talking* to him, the way you and I would talk. I'm trying not to listen, and it's making me feel funny, but what this guy's saying, real quietly, is stuff like, 'O.K., Sarge, we drove a long

3

way out here, now I sure hope you're not going to embarrass me' — just talking to him real gently and kind and quiet — and I'm trying not to listen, but I'm also getting kind of interested, kind of eager to see what kind of dog this Sarge is, that you can talk to like a person, instead of a dog.

"Well, we get out and walk a ways, and Sarge kind of cuts up, blows a point, and misses another, and the man was just getting all pained, writhing and flinching. Every time Sarge messed up, he'd take him aside and have another talk with him — I could hear him saying, 'Sarge! You're embarrassing me!' — and finally, when it just wasn't getting any better, the man, all sweating and upset, asked if he could have some more words with Sarge, alone.

"They got in their truck and drove down the road a ways — I thought they were leaving — and then they stopped under a shady tree — I could see them sitting there, talking — and after a while the guy drives back, still looking all pained, and he says to me, 'Sarge and I had a little talk down at the gate and we decided it's best for Sarge to stay here for a while.' "

All summer, I still didn't know if I'd done the right thing. The house seemed empty, the yard seemed haunted, without Colter. The older hounds, Homer and Ann, were thrilled, I think, that the newcomer, the upstart and thief of affection, had been sent away, that things had turned back to the way they used to be.

Oh, the wretched excess of the heart! Once a month, through the summer, I would fly to Texas and meet my father in Houston. We'd drive toward Austin, to Jarrett's farm, and turn down his long red clay driveway just at dawn. There is a little bluff, a fault line, slanting through Rosanky like a thin ribbon of scent, which allows pine forests to flourish in an otherwise scrub-brushy country, and we would drive past the big pines, and past all the dogs leaping in their kennels and barking, and Jarrett would greet us with a cup of coffee. He began all his days early in the spring and summer. It was important to work the dogs before the sun got too high and the heat burned the dew off the grass and made it hard for the dogs to smell the birds.

Each time, Jarrett would show me Colter's progress. And each time, I would be amazed at the finesse, the precision of execution required from a pointing dog. It has to learn so many things, and *execute*, every step of the way. Finding and pointing the bird is easy — it comes naturally. Working within range can be taught, eventually. But teaching the dog not to run after the bird when the bird flushes — not so easy. How to teach an animal to want something, but then, when the thing flies, to *not* want it? And to teach it not to run after a bird if it bumps one by accident — and to not run after the bird when you shoot? Steady-to-wing, they call it; steady-to-shot. And finally, the greatest challenge, steady-to-wing-and-shot.

If he had been less of a dog I would have tried to train him myself, making mistakes the way I do when I take something apart and then try to put it back together. But at least I had the sense to know this was a living, breathing *talent* — not some car engine, or a watch — who was going to be with me for the next ten years or more, both of us hunting fifty, sixty days a year — and that he deserved better.

The realization that I had, against my usual odds and inclination, somehow done the right thing came not at once, but in small increments, like confidence. Throughout the course of the summer I'd been fantasizing about taking Colter out of school a little early, to start the September grouse season in Montana, but Jarrett said that he needed more work, that he was still in a learning transition — he was starting to make real progress, but it was a very critical time for him.

I would panic, thinking, *I just want my dog back.* I would panic, and wonder, What good is it to have a great dog if you can't hunt with him?

Nancy, I could tell, was also unhappy about Colter's long absence from the valley, though she didn't say anything about it to me. She did ask Elizabeth once, "Doesn't he love Colter anymore?" And Elizabeth just laughed . . .

He was getting so big and muscular — each time I went to visit him he looked more like some hardened old muscular male bird dog, with only one thing on his mind. Where was my adolescent goofy-gangling little pup? He would leap up and run to greet me as ever, but more briefly each time, before sliding past and prancing around Jarrett's four-wheeler, on fire to go out into the field and hunt, even if only for a half-hour or so, as he did every day. Every day.

"I really like this dog," Jarrett would say. "I see a lot of dogs, but I really like old Colter. I think you could make a great field trial champion out of him," he'd say, meaning that Jarrett could do it, if I'd let him keep Colter all year long.

"Oh, I'm real anxious to get him home and start hunting with him," I'd tell him every time, and Jarrett would nod and look down at the brown dog he was spending every day with, and starting to respect and love, and he wouldn't say anything, and I'd wonder at what a hard job it must be for him: at how it was hard, in a different way, for him, and hard for me — hard for everyone but Colter.

"Do you ever dream about bird hunting?" I asked Jarrett.

"All the time," he said.

"Me too," I said, comforted that Jarrett, after a lifetime, still dreamed of it — that I have that to look forward to; that this was not love's first flush, but the real thing.

"Do you think the dogs do?" I asked.

"I'm certain of it," said Jarrett.

A bittersweet, lonely, early autumn of hunting grouse in my valley, the Yaak, with Tim and Maddie, but no Colter. Barely able to wait another day. Leaves turning color — no Colter! — and then, even worse, falling from the branches, and still no Colter there to see it with me, to taste it and smell it, to hunt it, each day.

Deer and elk season begins: a blessed relief. I disappear into the snow and fog.

And then one day Jarrett says Colter is ready — that he can take a little break, that it's the end of his session — but that he wants to see him back next year.

I go south one more time to pick up my dog. On the plane, my secret feels delicious: I am the richest man in the world, I have the greatest, most exciting dog in the world, and all around me, people are fooling with their coffee and ordering little cups of yogurt and reading their damn newspapers, while I have a bursting secret, and with pheasant season still open in Montana. Everyone else is stumbling around in the airport as if they don't seem to know that the world, and my heart, and the dog's heart, are on fire.

Two

A<small>LL</small> of my dogs have been wonderful accidents that have happened to me and now I am drowning in dogs and it is wonderful. I go to sleep amid the sounds of dogs stirring, settling in for the night downstairs, and wake up in the early morning to their whimpers and yawns and stretches. Of the first two dogs I ever owned as an adult, one, Homer, is still with me after fifteen years. Homer and Ann were black and tan Mississippi hounds of some unpatented beagle and walker hound and black and tan mix. When I found them, they were mangy and worm-ridden, and I only meant to take them to the animal shelter.

I was driving down a back road in Mississippi at dusk when I saw two tiny pups, one slender, one heavy, sitting by the roadside next to a third pup lying dead in the road. The slender pup, wild as the wind, galloped up a narrow game trail, arched with thorns and brambles of blackberry bushes, leapt up onto the splintered porch of an old abandoned house, and darted through an open door, disappearing into the dark maw of ruin.

I followed cautiously. I searched each room, half-fearing that humans, under the most dire of straits, might still be camping in that rubble, but each room was empty. When I came to the back porch, I saw that it opened out into the exuberant jungle of Mississippi in June. (The pups appeared to have just been weaned, seven weeks, which would place their birth sometime around Easter.)

I marveled at the slender pup's speed and wildness, imagining what it must have been like for that little wild thing to leap from the back porch down into that brambly thicket. A little sadly, I turned and went back to my truck, to the other pup still waiting by the roadside.

No matter, I told myself; a pup wild as that slender one — more of a coyote, really — wouldn't have made a very good pet anyway.

I got in the truck with the heavy pup, who wagged her tail and blinked her long eyelashes at me, ecstatic, and I drove on down the road.

With what subtle assuagements does landscape sculpt our hearts, our emotions; and from that catalyst, sometimes, our actions? I followed the winding road through the dusk tunnel of soft green light, and as I passed by the same place, a couple hundred yards down the road, where I'd first felt the impulse to turn around and go back for the pups, I felt it again. It was a feeling, a change, as dramatic as if I had passed through a doorway, and into an entirely different room. *You know,* I thought, *I ought not to split those little pups up like that.*

I turned around at about the same spot in the road and went back to give it one more try.

When I pulled back up to the abandoned house, the slender pup, Homer, was sitting out on the side of the road, in the same place where she had been earlier. I stopped the truck and jumped out, at which point she whirled and bolted, scampered up the viney trail and right back into the dark old falling-down house. I hurried after her, and once more went from room to room, looking for a tiny frightened wild pup, but found nothing, only decay. And once more I came finally to the back porch, with its storm-sprung doorless frame yawing straight into the gloom of jungle beyond.

What a pup, I marveled. *What a wild thing, making that four-foot leap into thorn and bramble. Too wild,* I thought again sadly, though my sorrow was tempered by the pleasure of having salvaged the one sweet little pup, and I returned to the truck knowing somehow that she would make a wonderful pet for someone; and, as before, she was thrilled to see me: thrilled to be petted, belly-thumped, noticed. Not yet loved, but noticed.

It was just before dark. I drove on down the road; and, amazingly, as I passed through that same invisible curtain — a curve of landscape, a mosaic of forest, and an open field beyond — I had the same feeling I'd had both times before. *There's still just a little bit of light left; I ought to try one more time. I ought to use up that last little bit of light trying.*

I turned around and went back to the old house. And again, the little hound was perched out front, roadside.

This time when she saw my truck she whirled and ran for the house even before I'd stopped; but I was quick, this time, and leapt from my truck and crossed the road in long strides, and hurdled the sagging, rusted iron gate, and plowed through the brambles, gaining on the pup.

She scampered up the steps and into the house. I was close behind, and this time I went straight to the back, hoping to catch her before she made that amazing leap.

But not quite. I was just a little too late, for when I came to that blasted-out doorway, again there was nothing but space, emptiness, and jungle beyond. The evening's first fireflies were beginning to cruise, as if sealing over the space into which the little hound had leapt, in the same manner with which the rings on a pond settle out to flatness, sealing over a stone that has been tossed into the pond's center.

Foiled again, and feeling a little foolish, a little defeated, and anxious to get on over to Elizabeth's before it got to be too late, I turned to go back to my truck, and to the one waiting puppy, again.

I was halfway down the hallway — the disintegrating shack eerie, ominous, in the failing light — when a new thought occurred to me: as if it had taken a shift in lighting to shove away an old assumption, and yield — tentatively, cautiously, at first — a new perspective.

That back-porch leap would be a heck of a jump for an animal as small as that pup to make; and to be making it again and again, so *relentlessly*: well, wasn't that a bit much? And how was she getting all the way out to the front of the house again so quickly, each time, after being swallowed by the jungle?

In all my previous explorations, I'd only glanced in each room. There was only the dullest blue light remaining, here and there, in the house. Dusk's first stars visible through the cracks and rips in the roof. Owls calling.

I went from room to room, checking behind the old moldering cardboard boxes of pots and pans, and rotting clothes, and mildewed ancient magazines, fast on their way to becoming humus. In each room, nothing, until I got to the last room — a wild clutter of yellowing newspapers — where I noticed what I had not before, a littering of small, dried-out twists of dog dung. As if they had been living in this room for quite some time.

There was a pile of loose sheets of newspaper over in the far corner of the room, by the window, and in the dim light, I could see that the papers were rattling slightly, as if from a breeze. I stepped over to the corner and lifted the sheets of paper, and there she was, tinier than I had remembered, and no longer fierce or barksome, and no longer any super dog, capable of great and daring leaps of escape, but instead a quivering, terrified little pup.

She was warm when I picked her up, and this time she did not resist. I tucked her in against my body and carried her out into the night to rejoin her sister.

Cows were lowing in the fields, a summer sound, when I arrived at Elizabeth's farmhouse. Steam was drifting in from off of the bayou.

"What are you going to do with them?" Elizabeth asked.

"Oh, I'll take them to the animal rescue league tomorrow," I said — never dreaming or imagining otherwise — though a short time later, as we watched them crouch bowlegged in front of a pan of milk and gulp at it until their bellies were stretched thumping tight, their tails wagging, it must have occurred to me, just the faintest shadow of a thought at first, *Well, I guess I could wait a day or two . . .*

Homer was named for the orphan Homer Wells, in John Irving's novel *The Cider House Rules,* which I was reading at the time. There was something about her slender elegance, even in her temporary disarray — patchy fur, burrs, etc. — that told me she was feminine enough to carry such a name, and to turn it from the masculine to the feminine.

Ann was named for Orphan Annie.

They slept in a cardboard box together — under a thin sheet, their heads tucked against each other's

14

shoulders. They slept soundly, not whining at all the way most pups do, but snoring slightly — as if completely content, now that they had finally gotten to where they needed to be. Having given them a little milk, and assigned them names, how could I turn them away?

I held them tiny in my hands. I followed them as if through a door, and nothing was ever the same. By stopping four, five minutes and picking up those sweet, funny, vulnerable little hounds, I stepped off the train tracks of my old life and into a slightly different world, where I stood at peace at the edge of shadows and sun dapple.

When we moved to Montana the dogs were depressed at first, missing Mississippi; they lay by the back door of the cabin for a solid month. But they grew accustomed to the new country and fell in love with life again. They went for hikes with me, chased the coyotes out of the yard, learned the new scents, new routines. They became mountain dogs soon enough; they refashioned themselves, out of loyalty. They learned about snow, about the values of a spot by the fireplace on a cold evening and the glories of muddy spring. They learned how certain things were backwards here, such as the geese leaving in the autumn, rather than arriving.

What else was there to do but adjust, and to love life?

I would often observe their loyalty, and watch their pleasure in this new place in the world, and try, in some units of measurement not yet known to man, to quantify the distance they had come, from being at death's door in Mississippi to chewing on a moldering old elk skull outside the cabin in Montana.

And I realized, soon enough, that that distance for them was the same distance for me.

Three

ONE of the great things about childhood — or so I remember it — was that everything you did was unquestioned by the self. Your every action — even those grounded in deceit — was pure, untainted by doubt or the foreknowledge of certain flaws that made you operate as you did. It never once occurred to me, for instance, to question why I felt so at home with the natural world and the ways of animals. The ways of adults were certainly off-limits to me, mysterious and, frankly, uninteresting (to a large degree, I fear, they still are), and even the companionship of my friends seemed relatively undependable and unintensifying.

Long before I became fully hostage to a life of reading, I was attracted to books like Fred Gibson's *Old Yeller* and *Savage Sam* and Sterling North's *Rascal* and *The Wolfling*, books that bore witness to (and glorified) the depths and breadth that the man-animal bond could reach. I had already felt the unmistakable and again comforting presence of grace when in the company of animals, especially wild animals: the stirrings of what Edward O. Wilson has labeled "biophilia" — our attachment to all living things. Best of all, there seemed to be no pecking order in the partaking of this grace; a child could have every bit as full a portion as an adult could. It wasn't a case of the woods allotting only a half-dose of their magic to children; no two-for-one days.

Back then, there were no questions as to *why:* no haggard midlife self-doubts, no self-pitying mopes that perhaps one reason I needed the woods so intensely was that I was so ill-suited to the world of man. Back then it was just sweet and clean and wild and fresh; and on many days, most days, the best days, it still is: and when I am in the company of one of my dogs, and am speaking to him or her as I would to a human friend — just shooting the shit or conversing about how the day has gone — or when I am admiring the sunlight in their eyes, or patting their heads, marveling at the physiographic fit between the curve of the palm of my hand and the top of their broad heads — as if we, or someone, has sculpted them just for that fit — or perhaps someone has sculpted *us,* for that fit — on those occasions, I do not concern myself with my inability to feel such comfort amidst humans (other than with a very few friends and family), but, rather, am simply thankful that at least dogs exist, and I'm humbly aware of how much less a person I'd be — how less a human — if they did not exist.

I don't mean to say that a human without a dog is somehow less of a human. What I mean is that I think there are those among us who are more dog people than others — and a dog person without a dog is missing something.

I don't care to enter into the genes-versus-experience tussle, as to what makes someone a hunter or a dog person, much less what makes someone be both, except that I will say I suspect that, viewed across a broad enough scale of time and distance, landscape, and the experiences that are shaped by landscape, *are* a kind of gene or chromosome: or at least they influence the development of genes so dramatically that landscape, and the cultures and experiences that spring forth from each particular landscape, might as well possess its own genetic code.

When I was a child, for whatever reasons, my hunting had not yet manifested itself, but my gathering certainly had. And I think this speaks to a more universal need or presence in us all — gathering, even hoarding — whose selective advantages are obvious.

The first things I keyed upon were, quite naturally, the animals that I could find along the Buffalo Bayou in the forested suburbs of Houston. These were mostly reptiles and amphibians: skinks, box turtles, false chameleons, leopard frogs, hognose snakes, snapping turtles, soft-shelled turtles, mud turtles, musk turtles, red-eared sliders, green snakes, forest toads, garter snakes, crawdads, bullfrogs, tree frogs, pollywogs, hellbenders. I collected with exuberance and totality, bringing home almost everything I could get my hands on, and releasing them into the assorted outdoor terrariums or aquariums in my back yard (the turtles I let run wild in the yard, like dogs or cats). It was an effort, I see now, to more fully surround myself with the citizens, the inhabitants of that other land, the woods, where I felt most full.

Again, with the innocence of childhood, not even tempted to analyze what came naturally, I was unaware that anything was amiss with regard to my social skills — though looking back now, I can see clearly the immensity of my separation from the world of my peers. Every spare moment was spent tromping about in the exploration, pursuit, and gathering of elusive living things; or, when the weather was too stormy, reading about the exploration, pursuit, and gathering of elusive living things.

We lived between the city and the country. The intensely urban war zone of Houston lay to the east, swathed most mornings in refinery haze, while to the west lay the oak woodlands and black loam prairie, not yet developed into the suburbs such as the one in which I grew up.

I always headed west, riding my bike each day to the place where the roads ended — the sparkling new cul-de-sacs — and disappearing into the woods. And from the very beginning, I was drawn to the elemental as many children are: I collected not only reptiles and amphibians, but feathers, stones, fish, plants, snakeskins, birds' nests — and, what at the time seemed like the most natural thing in the world to me, and only now do I realize how unusual it must have seemed to my family and friends — I collected dirt.

I didn't really worship it, not consciously, but the

edges of my bookshelves and desk and tabletops were lined with little glass and plastic vials and canisters of dirt: not just dirt from every place I had ever been, labeled with Dymo-tape, but dirt that my parents, as well as their friends and acquaintances had obtained for me. Dirt from Bangkok, Venezuela, China, Russia, India, and my grandmother's trip to Mexico City; dirt from Washington State, Oklahoma, New York City, and Michigan in winter, clawed frozen from beneath deep snow.

Collecting dirt for me became a game for my parents and their friends. My father was in the oil business, and his associates would travel far and wide, and I imagine that after a while it was no problem at all for him to ask someone heading out on a foreign trip, even someone he'd just met for the first time, "Oh, will you bring back a little dirt, a little soil, for my son Richard? He has a dirt collection."

Inevitably, I presume, a brief, amused interrogation would ensue. *Is it for a school project? No? He's doing it on his own. It's not an assignment? Well, what does he do with the dirt? He just looks at it? Touches it, and smells it? Well, all right — yes.*

I find it touching now in retrospect that these busy corporate men, en route to one important meeting after another (forty years later, were those meetings really more important than the dirt?) would take time to bag a little dirt and deliver it to me. I am touched by the spark of energy such an outlandish request must have brought to the routine of their lives, and I am touched too by my parents' pleasure at involving an ever-expanding network of friends and even strangers into the game.

From far and wide, the dirt came flying back to Houston, where it would be handed over to my father with pride, and always, a story: the "mule" nearly always having encountered a balky or disbelieving inspection agent in customs, a dubious or even impatient pilot. This was back in the days before there was much airline security, and no small number of the stories involved the businessman, having forgotten his mission right up until the very last moment — hearing the props begin to warm up, for the return trip home — running to the front of the plane and asking the pilot to hold on for a minute, and then clambering down the steps and dashing out across the tarmac to scoop up, in a handkerchief, a wad of marsh mud from Flanders or a daub of marl from Alberta.

As if delivering some incredibly potent, even illicit, substance, smuggled clear across the world by luck and cunning, the businessmen would with bright pleasure hand over the booty to my father, who would bring it home to me that evening, to my acquisitive rapture: loose clods of dried clay wrapped still in handkerchiefs, soil rattling in plastic bags, wisps of sand sifting from the edges of envelopes. Usually the samples were quite small — my father had explained the logistics of the collection — but I remember one time receiving a five-pound sack of white beach sand from Cozumel, dense as a bag of coins; I emptied the excess out in the street, where the winds and rains carried it, I suppose, out to the bayou, and from there, to the Gulf — drawn homeward, perhaps, I like to imagine, like iron filings seeking a magnet . . .

Whenever friends of my parents came over for bridge games they would invariably seek me out and ask me, in that cheery way that adults have with children in such circumstances — overjoyed at having a common ground of discussion — "How is your dirt collection going?" And occasionally a few of them would even wander back to my room to inspect it, alive again to the echoes and memories of childhood — venturing as close as they dared back to that country, that time and place, and always, they looked first to see where their donation was housed, still prideful in its gathering. I think that there is at least a little bit of hunter left in all of us.

I gathered nearly everything in those days, long before I ever dreamed I'd be gathering, or attempting to gather, birds to eat, birds found and gotten with my sweet dog.

I gathered crawfish from mud puddles the color of chocolate milk by tying a piece of raw bacon to a string and tossing it out into the murk, then reeling it in slowly, with a whole armada of long-whiskered crustaceans trailing slowly behind it, pincers waving. I splashed out into ponds blindly, waving my dipnet at darting, flashing schools of minnows, then lifted them thrashing and flopping silver-sided in the sun, feeling flush with the great bounty of each filled dipnet — and then I let them go. I had not yet turned the corner on hunting. It was in me all along, but I was not yet in it.

*   *   *

As a child, I was wild not so much about dogs, but about turtles. I have no idea what it was about them that drew me so; at the time, I would have known nothing of the archetypal values ascribed to them, such as endurance and world genesis. I was especially wild about the gothic grotesqueries of snapping turtles. I adored their savage appetites, was fascinated by their infinite belligerence, and took awed solace in their hideous land-bound clumsiness, for here was a creature, a dinosaur really, that appeared supremely dispossessed in the world — unglamorous, unfriendly, even plain plug-ugly — and yet it thrived like a king, seeking out the muddy depths where other turtles could not prosper or would not go. The larger ones, I had read, could measure over three feet long, and might weigh in excess of a hundred pounds. They were eaters of fish, snakes, other turtles, and even ducks. It was said that their bite was powerful enough to snap a broomstick in two, or to sever a finger, and that once they bit they would not turn loose until thunder boomed. The true behemoths never came to the surface, I'd heard, except once a year to breed and lay eggs, but I would occasionally luck onto one of their smaller progeny, which made the most satisfying, aggressive pets. They ranged in size from a golf ball to a frying pan, and even the smallest gave pause to an observer, with their baleful red eyes and hissing malevolence. Though I never saw one of the true giants in its depths, it was a source of great pleasure to me to know that they were down there, secure in their element, titanic.

The one time I did see a giant snapper, it was not in

its element, but in transition. I viewed it for only a few moments, but what a glorious and heart-rending few they were.

I was twelve or thirteen years old, in the full grip of my collecting ways, and my turtlemania. Some weekends my parents would travel out toward the town of Katy, in the prairie, which was then only a hamlet, rather than the sterilized suburban strip mall it has since become. They played golf at a club called Jersey Village, only recently carved out of prime bayou woodland, and it was one of my great joys to be allowed to fish and dipnet in the water hazards of the golf course, as long as I stayed out of the way of the golfers.

I've never experienced better fishing in my life, nor a more exhilarating general fecundity. The bass and bream bit harder and fought better, as did the sleek potbellied catfish. There were giant bullfrogs everywhere, and great populations of pollywogs, entire nests of snakes (and not just the sissy little garter snakes, but water moccasins, too, the real thing, dark as charred wood and as thick around as men's wrists). There were swirling inky swarms of newly hatched catfish fry, wandering chaotically across the surface in amorphous rafts made up of hundreds of individuals: a sight so exciting to me that when I saw it I would often leap fully clothed into the water with my dipnet, no matter the water's depth, hoping to net one of the half-inch catfish. (It was such an exciting and magical sight that I still dream of it to this day; the last time I dreamed it, my youngest daughter, four years old, was with me, and I was trying to explain to her what she was seeing, in the dream: that that clumsy, drifting loose wiggling sprawl was about five hundred newborn catfish all swimming together for protection, in their first few days of life . . .)

And there were, of course, turtles, of all possible species, in every possible size, and on a good day I might be fortunate enough to catch one. (It isn't as easy as you might think if you haven't tried it. Capturing the terrestrial box turtles was simple enough, but the aquatic turtles were quick as lightning, in the water.)

They couldn't resist basking, however, and I would slither on my belly toward a log on which ten or twenty of them might be perched, sunning themselves, frozen like statues. Crawling like a commando, hoping to evade the twenty pair of sentinel eyes, I would make a quick charge at the end, hoping to net the slowest one as they all slipped off the log into the water. When they hit the water they usually went straight to the bottom, but occasionally in its panic one would land upside down and might linger on the surface for half a second, righting itself, and that was when I had a chance, if the handle on my dipnet was long enough . . .

It was dusk, and storming, as it can storm only in the subtropics in late spring and early summer: violent bursts that tear green limbs from trees and flood streets and knock out power poles, dropping four or five inches of rain in a couple of hours, and above and through it all, the wonderful crackling and roaring of thunder and lightning.

We were driving out of the club in the downpour. As

we wound our way along the little road, beneath the boughs of ancient live oaks, I glanced out at one of the putting greens and saw, in the dimming light, the silhouette of my desire — the perfect shape of it manifested as if into archetype and then magnified tenfold: a snapping turtle that seemed to be the size of a small Volkswagen lumbering across that verdant lawn of civilization, tumultuous rain hammering against her shell as she dragged her immense bulk, nearly too great for the land to bear, from the depths of a pond up toward a sand trap, where she might be intending to lay her eggs. (I did not stop to think of that at the time; I knew only that by the most miraculous of flukes, I had sighted my life's quarry — a quarry I did not even know I had been pursuing until I saw it, creeping across that manicured grass, gargantuan and lovely in its hideousness.)

Even my parents were impressed. We stopped and viewed it from the car as we might the nearsighted rhinoceros or tame garbage-bears at some drive-through safari park, and then I was out the door and running toward the turtle, and my parents snatched up their umbrellas and bailed out of the car and came running after me.

As I joined the massive turtle she hunched upon her hind legs, hissed and spat, but then trudged on resolutely, making good time for such a labored and ponderous gait, dragging that huge spiny tail behind her like a log.

Her feet were broad as a wolf's, with claws like a bear's. Had she not been so ferocious, I would have tried riding on the back of her shell, as I had sometimes done with the immense but gentle Galápagos tortoises at the zoo.

It was her head that was most spellbinding. It was easily the size of a man's head; and her eyes were as large as oversized marbles. The three of us were mesmerized by this strange new inhabitant of the earth, and I pleaded with my parents to let me take it home. I could tell they sympathized with the immensity of my discovery, but they realized also the impossibility of caring and feeding for such a monstrosity in the suburbs, and they were adamant in their refusal.

I sobbed in anguish as we tracked the great creature on her charmed and steadfast path. "We could put her in the trunk," I pleaded, and even grabbed hold of her long tail in an attempt to show my father that it was possible, that she *could* be transported.

This was a mistake. With a savage hiss she jacked her hind end up and dug deep in the turf with those powerful forelegs, and quick as a ferret whirled and snapped at me: I was barely able to release the tail and leap back in time. She had the power of a sumo wrestler and the speed of a rattlesnake.

I took another step back and watched as she reoriented herself with whatever magnetic tack she had been following, and then once more, with thunder booming and lightning flashing and rain howling, we resumed following her. My parents were holding up their umbrellas in vain attempts to stay dry in the storm, and as the three of us walked in procession behind and flanking the astounding reptile, it might have seemed to a distant observer that we were exercising the animal, taking it for a walk on a leash, or perhaps even being pulled by it. Glimpsed between lightning bolts, as darkness fell quickly now, we would have looked like characters from the Addams Family, and I suspect a passerby would not have been inclined to stop and ask if we needed any help . . .

We followed her all the way to another flood-swollen pond, into which she disappeared gratefully — as gracefully, I could see in that last boom of lightning-flash, as a ballerina. I was still crying in my frustration, still arguing with my parents right up until the very end, and I recall being very angry at them for a long time, though by now I have completely forgiven them. And I've never forgotten the wild power and savagery of that sudden head strike, when I gripped the turtle's tail.

Myths and creation stories tell us that turtles were here before the world was; that turtles formed the world: that their shells were the firmament upon which all subsequent terrestrial life grew. Turtles may not be that old, but they are far more ancient than hominoids and dogs, and humans have certainly known turtles far longer, if less intensely, than they have known dogs, even though recent science is showing that dogs and humans have had a bond and a relationship probably since early men rose to a crouch and walked semi-upright. There's no real telling what the nature of the relationship was, going so far back into the murky past — did we scavenge off the leavings of wild-dog kills? What did the dogs get in return from us? Why the bond? Why do they help fulfill our need to love, and be loved, and do they possess a similar need?

Scientists hypothesize about the symbiotic nature of the relationship, then as well as now, but anyone who's ever known a dog of even moderate personality knows that the relationship is not simply about food, or any other of the cruder biological necessities of survival: that there is something interior, something luminous, a spirit yet invisible to the world, in the bond between people and dogs.

As "plastic" as dogs are emotionally — so willing to please us — so too, apparently, are they willing to please us genetically. Genetic research has shown, for example, that every dog in the world has descended from one ancestor, and that only through our selective breeding have we crafted and sculpted — like little gods — the amazing variety of dogs we see today. The Mexican chihuahua, for instance, was bred in response to the overflow of human fecal material on city streets in medieval times. Humans identified dogs that liked to eat human shit, bred them short-haired so the feces didn't get caught in their fur, then turned them out into the streets, like terrestrial vultures. For good measure, they bred the bark out of them, since these little scrubbers wouldn't be watchdogs, wouldn't really be anyone's dogs.

Whatever we desired, we would take the fire in their hearts and breed it and bend it in the direction of our own desires — and dogs allowed us to do this; they accepted the shapes our hearts and minds dreamed for them. My magnificent Colter, for instance, is of a

breed refined only in the last century, though his pre-
decessors, pointing dogs in general — those dogs that
indicated a tendency to pause, in the presence of hidden game — foredated him by many centuries.

When you live with a dog — when a dog is a member
of your family — you learn soon enough to see the
world at least partially through that dog's eyes: when
to let it out, when to let it in, when to feed it, when it
wants to play, when it is troubled . . .

With a hunting dog, you learn to pursue what it pur-
sues. Generations of mankind before you might have
worked to sculpt this streamlined (yet fluid, and still
developing) creature that is now in your life, and now,
not in generations but in just a few short years, the dog
turns around and sculpts you.

It's very strange. I accept that sculpting gladly, gratefully.

Four

COLTER'S PARENTS, Tom and Nancy, live in a cabin by the river. Tom traps. He and Nancy tan the hides in a smoke-filled tent, rather than sending them out to be chemical-tanned. The hides they tan make a much thicker, and infinitely softer leather. They sew the leather into clothes, moccasins, gloves.

"It's damned good to feel your woman through one of these," Tom'll say, with a twinkle in his eye, when I exclaim over the softness of a hide.

When I moved here thirteen years ago Tom was in his late forties, which means now he's pushing sixty. But he doesn't seem to be getting any older. He's limping a little, this year, after a knee operation, but otherwise he and Nancy don't seem to have changed a bit.

Visiting them in their cabin high above the river looking out across at the mountain is calming and magical. What does it say about the way we live now, that a cabin filled with the most elemental and physical of objects — stone, bone, wood, antler, feather, fur — seems imaginary, fantastic, almost surreal? Mounted Canada geese hang suspended from the ceiling, as if still soaring. A mounted buffalo head — a bull — stares down woolly-headed. Antlered skulls of deer and elk line the log walls. The plank flooring shines smooth-worn in lantern light. The dogs — Paggon, Colter's mother, and Jaeger, his younger brother — sleep groaning and snoring in a nest by the wood stove, as content as dogs know how to be, which is considerable.

There's no one who can baby a dog like Nancy. She carried Colter, held him, every day for the first couple of months of his life, until he came to me — at which point I did the same. And from Nancy's unconditional and unremitting love comes, I'm convinced, a foundation upon which the dog can rest, serene and confident, from the first day of puppyhood through the last day of old age.

Before Colter, I hunted only big game — skulking through the rainy, and then snowy, November woods, following, or hoping to intercept, deer and elk.

To enter the world of bird hunting — to have the quarry leap into the bright sky, rather than bounding off into the brush, or into the fog — and to have a magician alongside and in front of me who would always reveal where the quarry lies . . . it was like passing through a door, one I didn't even notice was there, into a place of light and beauty.

Five

Mʏ ʙᴏʏ, my brown boy Colter — named for the mountain man who outran a whole tribe of Blackfeet — is a year and a half old. He's proven himself a genius on grouse, and now I'm going to give him his first shot at pheasants. He and Tim Linehan's six-year-old golden retriever, Maddie, ride nestled together in the back of Tim's truck. It's cold — somewhere just this side or the other of zero — but sunny, by God; we find sun less than an hour into our journey, and don't look back.

We drive up and over the Continental Divide, somewhere east of Glacier: the world falls away before us. We ride down out of the mountains without speaking, merely gaping at the flat eastern country below, and blue sky, and sunshine. It doesn't matter what town we head to — they are not all the same, but they are all similar.

We check into the only motel in town, where we're the only guests. Because it's so damn cold, the potholes are frozen over, and there are no duck hunters around. No other pheasant hunters either; the sensible ones did their shooting in the warm months, October and November.

Tom will join us in a couple of days, but for now it's just Tim and me and Colter and Maddie. Tim loves his dog as much as I love mine.

Here is how it is done, according to Tom: you just go up to a farmhouse and knock on the door. You ask if you can hunt on the farmer's land. When the door opens, usually — according to Tom — they say yes. It's like Halloween, like trick-or-treat for grown-ups.

We've got an hour of light left and we drive out of town and stop at the first farmhouse we see, a stark white house surrounded by the bare limbs of a December windbreak. A woman answers the door. It's too cold and windy to stand there with the door open, so she invites us in immediately, and, learning we are hunters, she takes us into the den and shows us the buck her husband shot last year. We ask if we can hunt pheasants on her land and she says yes, and we shake hands and head back out into the wind and cold. The sun is very low on the horizon now, but it is still undeniably sun. The forecast calls for sixty- to seventy-mile-an-hour gusts, later in the night, with wind chill down to around fifty below.

We drive across the road to a field of uncultivated land, put the grouse bells on the dogs, load our guns, and step into the ankle-high grass.

The dogs rocket into the wind, as if locked in twin harness: no casting, no weaving. They run north without looking back. They disappear. There's nothing to do but push on after them, to the North Pole if need be. After a while they come back to join us. Maddie catches the gist of it first and flushes a hen pheasant, and then another. The sun's slipping lower and our hands hurt from the cold, even in heavy gloves. The dogs take off to the north again, running a bird that will not flush and will not let itself be pointed; they disappear once more, perhaps running over into Canada. It gets dark, and colder than iron; we turn around and head back to the truck, shivering. The dogs catch up with us, and we drive back to the motel room.

"Damn, that was fun," says Tim. We have a leisurely supper — fried eggs, sausage, pancakes, coffee — at the Bobcat Café next door; the bill for both of us totals seven dollars. We retire to the room and watch a nature special on dolphins, filmed somewhere down in the tropics. We don't get television in the Yaak. We live in cabins with wood stoves for heat, which we must tend to in the middle of the night, but this motel room is toasty warm, while outside, the world freezes.

That night I dream I am crouched over a block of crystalline ice with hammer and chisel and am tapping and tapping. I find a cleft and the shell ice splits into two halves. I expect there to be a pheasant, a rooster, within that crystal, but there is only bright light, sunlight, and it is enough.

*   *   *

I've brought a spark collar, shock collar, behavioral correction unit, whatever you want to call it, with me, to keep Colter from running over the horizon — and I have got it plugged into the wall socket, charging, but sometime in the night it falls out, or Colter gets up and unplugs it, so that we will have to hunt naked. I am secretly relieved; I've never used it on him before.

We knock on more doors that morning, and everyone says yes — says hell yes — and we find pheasants. Colter's not locking down on the scent yet — he's not pointing — but he's sure finding the birds, weaving wildly and joyously through the thick grass, bounding in goofy pogo leaps like a mule deer, or a fox pouncing on a mouse — head swiveling this way and that, delirious on the jetstream of myriad scents, hundreds of birds running, scuttling, and the ringing of the dogs' bells, and the distant shouts of Tim and me trying to call our dogs back . . . Sometimes the flushed birds fly back toward us rather than away, so that we're able to get a shot, but we're shooting like shit and the birds just keep on flying, all morning long — some of them roosters, big roosters. One of them seems as large as a pterodactyl — Colter locks down on him, a perfect point — but I am so surprised by the bird's immensity, and the proximity of him, that I miss both shots.

Jarrett Thompson had worked with Colter on bobwhite that summer — had trained him, even in his adolescence, to be steady to shot — but there in the field, with Tim and I running and shouting, and with no birds dropping — every bird flying away, every damn one of them, not at all like Jarrett's training school — well, there in the field, things unravel. The pterodactyl-pheasant veers and flies toward a distant abandoned farmhouse, squawking, laughing.

We spend the rest of that sunny, frigid morning wandering around one of the great square fields, trying to keep the wind always in our faces, even when the dogs are no longer in sight. Colter is still jumpy, twitchy, anticipating the flushes — after each flush he runs after the bird, barking madly — but sweet and elegant Maddie is beginning to work closer, so that we're learning to read her body language: the propeller-like spinning of her thick banner of a tail when she is trailing a running bird — the "spin-move," like Hakeem Olajuwon in the paint, when the running rooster reverses direction on her, or when she hears or even sees it; and the double-paw pounce — again, like a fox on a mouse under the snow, when she flushes the bird — but still, we are missing, missing, missing.

Sound carries a long way, out in the flatlands; much farther than what we're used to back in the alder and aspen jungles, the creeks and swales of fir and spruce in the Yaak. We see a couple of ladies riding horses a mile or so distant, driving a loose herd of cattle down the dusty road before them, Border collies at the herd's flank, and our hearts swell with the undeserved glory of our predicament: at full play in mid-December, while the rest of the world works hard.

I look down and see that Colter has returned and has gone on lock-solid, drop-dead point about twenty feet in front of us, head and shoulders hunched and crouched, bony ass stuck way up in the air, body half-twisted, frozen, as if cautioning us of some hidden, deadly betrayal: and green eyes afire, stub tail motionless.

We ease forward, adrenaline-drunk. Nothing happens. And then it does. The cock-bird climbs towering above and then flares and accelerates away; Tim fires twice, I fire twice, Colter runs shrieking after the untouched bird, and from across that spartan landscape we hear the cattlewomen snort small laughs of disbelief, and one of them says, "*Oops,* they missed again."

We continue to be greeted at farmhouse front doors with unimaginable courtesy and hospitality. We try to remember the names of our benefactors, and jot down their addresses on scraps of napkins and paper bags, afterward; but in our enthusiasm for the hunt, in the mind-scrambling, mind-dumping, and reordering that goes on in the heat of the hunt, we usually end up forgetting the proper names and can speak of the coverts later that night in only a frantic, abbreviated shorthand: Red Barn Man. Happy Man. Hippie-Dude's Place. Pit Bull Cover, so named for the pit bull bitch that followed us from the farmhouse and out into the field and who kept nipping at all four of us — Tim and me, and the two dogs — as we hurried after the running pheasants; nipping at young Colter even as he staunchly held point.

The great mountains — the Stony Mountains — shine white and blue in the near distance, like guardians over our mountain souls as we frolic down in the flatlands — land of monoculture, land of sun, land of fun. The scowling intensity of our deer season — the gray broodiness, the sneakiness — falls away into bright laughter.

It's a day of many misses — all misses, in fact — but of unrelenting grace. Colter pointed a skunk, but all parties escaped unscathed. At one point he is gone for an hour and returns with a single porcupine quill stuck in his lower lip.

Back in the warm motel room Tim and I share a six-pack, bragging on our dogs, and watch a football game on that strange small blue-glowing miracle, the television. We've gotten so charged-up, so oversensitized and overstimulated, out on the strange magic prairie, that we need something to suck our brains out and back down to zero — to counterbalance things — and the beer and television are just the thing.

The dogs lie resting on the bed, watching us watch the game, their eyes bright, waiting for tomorrow.

In the morning the Rockies are carved in ice, sculpted white with new snow, as are the Sweetgrass Hills to the north, though no snow fell down in the flatland. The sky is clear, as if that snow up in the hills and mountains was put there not by clouds, but by magic. Each of the three hills is burnished by the day's new light, a strange distant copper color touching only the snow hills, and they seem almost a place to look at, rather than go to: as if they contain too much power to be approached in a frivolous state of mind. A mining company out of Minneapolis wants to crush and pulp the hills for gold — sixty tons of rock per ounce of gold — and I can barely stand the thought of it, although I've only seen them this once from afar. What must it have been like for the Blackfeet, who lived beneath them and who came to the hills for purification and healing — gathering and burning bunches of sweetgrass to use as incense in sacred ceremonies, and to fast, build sweat lodges, and wait for visions; *to live*? What must it be like for them, to look at those hills? How could such a strong people, so attached to the blood rhythms of the earth, have been defeated by a culture as pale and pasty as our own?

We hunt around the missile silos that day. More birds, more shots, more misses. How can anyone miss anything as large as a pheasant? Colter and Maddie are both learning fast — Maddie trying to bend the running pheasants back toward us, or, if we're close enough, trying valiantly to make them flush right then and there, while Colter continues to freeze like a viper whenever he steps in that kill-zone of hot scent. So jazzed is the young pointer that, though he holds his points staunchly, as if cast in instant bronze, he has taken to screaming — not howling or yelping, but screaming — even as he holds that staunch point, and screaming louder than do the brightly colored birds with the long tails as they sail away unscathed, and the sounds of our presence echo and roll across the golden plains. There's so much shooting that I worry whether the security sensors around the silos are registering their alarm and red lights in Washington are glowing and beeping. Perhaps one more volley, one more fruitless fusillade, will send things over the edge, and the silo panels will fall away and the great doomsday rockets will emerge, lighting the sky orange and scorch-melting our flesh (the scent of cooked wheat all around us) — or perhaps Colter's panther-like screams will be enough to trip the signals and break the earth open below, cracking it in half and giving birth to the end of the world, all because we could not hit a pheasant . . .

That afternoon Colter points a short-eared owl in its stick-nest burrow on the ground. The bird refuses to flush, only hisses and clacks its beak at us.

Still later, he jumps a jackrabbit; both he and the rabbit are off to the races, moving so fast and in such a straight line across the horizon that they both seem to be drawn on a string, a fast string being sucked away into eternity . . . It's a lot of new stuff to throw at a young dog.

Who knows what combinations, what sequence and percentage of experience versus bloodline conspires to sculpt an individual? Perhaps by dint of his being the runt of the litter, unpicked until the very last, he developed an extraordinary drive — a fury to excel at the thing the world, and his blood, told him to do.

It's also possible that his extra weeks with Nancy, after all his other littermates had been adopted, had swelled his heart with such an excess of love that he came to believe in himself, and in the joy of the world, with such thunderous exuberance that for a long, long time he would not believe older, more faded, worldly notions such as boundaries, borders, or even restraint.

As if the world had been created only for him to hurl himself at, and beyond.

*   *   *

Just after dusk, making the long hike back to the truck, exhausted and birdless, with a full moon rising above the Sweetgrass Hills, we jump a big buck. His antlers are bone white, glowing in the moonlight: sun-bleached, out here on the plains, rather than the dark, deep-chocolate-colored antlers of the bucks we're used to seeing back in the jungle.

We're starting to drag. The dogs are covering over a hundred miles a day. We're getting lots of shooting practice. I think we're going to hit one soon.

Tom, perhaps the world's most skilled outdoorsman, joins us the next day. He has brought Paggon, Colter's mother. Tom promptly begins killing birds — hitting and dropping whatever he aims at — but we forgive him because he is such a good friend.

Tim and I don't understand that you're not supposed to hurry up to your dog when he's on point — that you're supposed to *saunter,* calling casual words of encouragement; that you're supposed to try to keep your heart to less than eighty beats per minute, to be calm and steady as you stroll up, with the world — all that you and your dog have been laboring for, all autumn, indeed, all of your lives together — frozen as if forever.

Tom shows us how it's done. I've got to admit, he makes it look pretty cool: striding to his destiny, rather than charging high-kneed and panting through the stubble, shotguns broken and held aloft for safety as Tim and I do, storming the hills toward the frozen dark brown dog as if intent upon taking a beachhead.

At lunch, Tom lights a cigar and tells us that he'd be

embarrassed if there was anyone around to see us. But there isn't. They've all gone south for the winter, for vacations in Billings, in Miles City, or the South Pacific. Farming is over till spring. The land lies silent, save for Colter's occasional screams.

Tom is a falconer; and as he follows Paggon along a creek bottom — Paggon's stub tail spinning furiously as she works sweet hot moving scent — a redtail hawk drifts down out of the blue sky like a falling oak leaf, just as Paggon goes on point, and when Tom moves in, a pheasant — a rooster — flushes straight up into the blue sky, but then folds its wings as Tom raises his gun. Before he can fire, however, the pheasant falls back to the ground, narrowly avoiding the hawk's plunge.

The pheasant bounces and is up and running again, with the hawk chasing it, Paggon barking and Tom hurrying behind. The hawk, foiled, flares away; the pheasant foolishly takes flight again, and Tom shoots it this time. The hawk lands in the top of a cottonwood and looks down and watches Tom and Paggon claim the bird.

Pheasant number three, a full limit; from now on, today, it'll have to be sharp-tail grouse or Hungarian partridges, for Tom. He smokes another cigar, looking very much at peace with the world.

Colter really wants a pheasant; so does Maddie. I don't care if I ever hit one or not — well, actually, that's not quite true — but I do want these incredible, wonderful, steadfast dogs to have one.

We drive down the road, searching for a new covert

to try. The mesh screen for the sliding window of Tim's camper shell flaps in the wind from where, on an earlier grouse hunt this fall, Colter, rather than remaining in the truck where we had left him (for disciplinary reasons) chose to chew his way out, and joined us — proudly — out in the woods (scaring the shit out of us as he came bounding up silently from behind, dark as a bear, fast as a lion . . .).

We stop at a homestead owned by a man we've named for the huge leaking plug of tobacco he keeps stored in his cheek as he talks. He has a little forty-acre piece up on the hill — we can identify it by the mass of rotting hay bales that rest at the bottom of the hill like a stinking ship, hay bales from the century before, perhaps — and he has more land too, he tells us, but those lands have coyote-getters scattered all around. Whether he means cyanide traps or explosive, baited cartridges buried just beneath the skin of the earth, I don't know, and don't ask. Tobacco Man advises us that we might want to keep our dogs away from those places, and we agree. We don't get into it with him — the studies that show that the harder you trap coyotes, the more offspring they produce and the younger the population becomes, and that its those young coyotes who are usually the troublemakers. We don't ask him why he's killing coyotes. He would tell us that they eat calves, as wolves once ate freely of the hundred million buffalo that used to pass through here.

Feeling troubled by the endless, useless war on coyotes, who would eat the rabbits and pheasants that eat the grass and grain that the cattle could otherwise eat, or the farmer could otherwise sell, we head over to the forty acres. The other dogs are a bit winded, so we run Colter solo.

Forgive me for bragging on my dog. Forgive me always for doing this. It is not meant to be any reflection upon myself, by any means, but rather, simply, an astonished marveling, a celebration, of my undeniable good fortune to be blessed, graced, by his all-encompassing talent.

He runs the fucking table. We point him downhill and into the wind. There are seven roosters in that forty acres and he points them all. The reason I know there were not eight is because he did not find eight.

He courses the field as if in a mad slalom, a giant, seven-legged Z — a canine Zorro, slashing innumerable smaller Z's with seeming abandon — reckless, until the moment, the point of truth with each bird, when he locks up solid, sometimes almost pitching forward in a somersault, so sudden is his stop — his hind legs and bony rear end almost piling up over his front legs, or swinging like a jack-knifed trailer way out around in front of him.

The birds hold; then they flush. We fire, and miss. We miss and miss, and it doesn't matter. In bird hunting, one piece of bliss — one little window of dog perfection, one wedge of success, thirty seconds of grace, is enough to obliterate all the errors of a lifetime — either yours, or the dog's.

By the bottom of the hill, Colter is trembling as he points, locked up on that seventh rooster. Streams of snow-white slobber trail from his jowls, fleck his face. *My dog;* I am so tired of letting him down.

The rooster flushes, flares left; I swing and shoot and keep swinging, and the bird tumbles almost inexplicably — so unaccustomed am I to this result — to the ground, a small cloud of feathers floating above him, marking his descent. Colter rushes over to the bird — we can see its copper and black feathers sticking up out of the brush where he has crash-landed — and sinks his inch-long fangs into the dead bird's breast and begins shaking the bird like a rat terrier, making more feathers fly. I hurry over and take the bird from him and pat him.

Tim and Tom are cheering, as happy for Colter as I am, and they come over to congratulate us, as if we have done something difficult, not simple: not blood-earth simple.

If the bird had flared right, Tim would have hit it.

A night of celebration. The three dogs wrestling on the bed, playing like puppies: aging mother, her young son Colter, and the elegant, peak-of-her-prime Maddie: three dogs writhing, yipping, panting, grinning — pouncing on one another and playing tag.

The weather report says there's still a blizzard going on, back up over the other side of the Divide — back in the dark woods.

The freezer is full of Tom's birds. There are pretty feathers everywhere; the dogs have ripped into the paper bag full of them that we have saved to take back home, to show our people what pheasants look like. Feathers on the tips of the dogs' noses, feathers all over their backs, all over the room.

*   *   *

The last day is even colder and more brilliant. Hoar-frost falling through the sky, sparkling in the midday sun. The hills so magical. Who could ever erase them? Why not outlaw oceans, or destroy the stars; why not ban the moon?

Midday, Maddie runs a rooster zigging and zagging through the pit bull covert; the bird erupts, flies right past Tim, and he fires and drops it: Maddie retrieves it. Tim is smiling, as quiet, as she brings it in to him, as I was exultant, yesterday — but I know he is feeling the exact same way, inside: the very same.

We hunt almost all the rest of the day, in that sun-glittery cold, stopping to marvel at the scenery often. When the dogs' vertebrae begin showing, we turn around and go back home, back across the prairie and up and over the pass, back into the heart of winter; but our blood is filled, once more, with sunlight and magic.

Six

COLTER WENT BACK to school the next summer, but for a short session — he was almost finished, almost perfect. Jarrett poured the birds to him, a labor of love — putting him through high repetitions, to maintain his great attributes — his unfettered athleticism, his speed, his desire, his nose — while whittling down, one bird at a time, his tendency to chase after a shot, or a flush. A lot of Colter's improvement that year came simply from the security, the confidence, of knowing that there was always going to be another bird, another hunt. He didn't scream nearly as much when he stood staunchly on point now.

Finally, late in August, he was ready. He'd learned all his lessons. All mistakes had been carved away by Jarrett in only two seasons. All that was left was a perfect, muscular, eager brown dog, still young, with his life before him: hundreds of hunts awaiting in the seasons beyond, and a multitude of species, a multitude of scents.

There was such a feeling of freedom, that last day: as if I were the one graduating, not Colter. My little man was coming home.

Jarrett took my father and me out into the field for one last training session. As always, he stressed that the dog was never the problem: that it was always the owners who were the slow learners, and who would make the mistakes, from here on out. He concentrated on watching me work Colter on the birds, rather than watching Colter. He'd been watching Colter all summer, and knew how he'd do.

"Be a little sterner with him," Jarrett kept cautioning. "He's like a teenager who's just gotten the keys to Dad's car. He'll try to test you."

Jarrett kept watching me as if we were both walking on eggshells. Watching to see whether I was going to be worthy of both the dog and Jarrett's investment — all his time, these last two summers, and also all his heart and hopes.

We came to a field where Jarrett had turned one bird loose. We watched silently as Colter scented it immediately and swung high-headed toward it like a horse being turned by sharp reins, knifing quickly, confidently, through the tall dry grass before crouching and freezing suddenly at the precise last place where he could travel without flushing the bird — which, in this case, was right on top of the bird.

"*Whoa*," I said. His tail was locked. The bird was there.

We stood there in the morning sunlight admiring

him, frozen in time: the morning mist rising from the ocher-autumn grass, the brown-muscled dog, the tall pines. To be in the presence of, to be at the side of, such power: it made my eyes glisten. The old world behind me seemed so much smaller and finite, compared to this new one.

I stepped up, nudged the clump of grass in front of Colter, and the little quail burst up in wing-rocketry and whirred away into the brush. Colter's eyes and nostrils flared wider, but other than that he made no move; Jarrett had trained him not to. There could be other birds hiding.

I released him — tapped him on the top of his beautiful head and said, "All right, good boy."

He broke from the trance and began working the field in front of us. Jarrett and my father and I let down a bit, knowing there were no more birds in that field — Jarrett had planted just one — and we walked on toward the next field, savoring the power and perfection we'd just seen.

"He's got something out there," my father said, looking back.

We turned and saw that Colter was on point again: not locked-down tail-stub-rigid point, but fierce enough — the stub twitching only so slightly, indicating that there wasn't quite a full bird there, but something very close to a full bird — the ghost scent, still warm, of where that bird had been — and I had a little sinking feeling, for I'd never known Colter to false-point before.

It wasn't quite a full point — not as long as his little nub was twitching — but he was still giving far too much interest to an old scent. We went over to where he stood and kicked at the grass in front of his nose.

"It's gone, boy," Jarrett said, but didn't release him yet, and Colter continued to stand his ground.

Then Jarrett saw something. He crouched and picked it up from beneath the grass, looked at it, and handed it to me. It was a single quail feather: one that must have pulled loose and floated free when the lone bird erupted from the grass minutes earlier. The downy feather blazed in the morning light. I took it from Jarrett and placed it in my wallet.

"You've got a good dog," Jarrett said — never one to get all gushy. "I sure wish he were mine. I'd love to use him as a guide dog on hunts with my clients down in south Texas this season. I think all he lacks is a little more experience with *wild* birds . . ."

It made me feel good, that Jarrett wanted Colter to be his star dog, and borrow him through the winter — putting him into new situations with wild birds, and racking up invaluable experience — but I said no, thank you. I couldn't stand being gone from him another minute.

Jarrett's face betrayed nothing, but I could feel the sadness in his heart as he began the letting go. As he'd had to do with hundreds of dogs, maybe thousands. But never one like this one. Still, he knew the drill. He went through it by rote.

We headed back to the farm, Colter bounding and casting in front of us: me joyous, my father impressed, and Jarrett silent, thinking ahead to the rest of his day's work.

Back at the house, Jarrett stressed for the umpteenth

time how important the transition would be, and how I couldn't let him break me, or he'd go back to ranging too far — the river running too wild, flooding its banks — and bumping birds.

I said I'd do my best. I knew that a dog like Colter could never be broken, and that I would always have to be prepared for him to test me, and to take off for the horizon.

Jarrett looked at me with what seemed like an infinite sadness.

"Oh, you can break him," he said. "It'll happen."

I laughed, but Jarrett didn't. "It may take a long time," he said, "but you'll win."

I couldn't figure out why he looked so sad, so haunted. I laughed again and tried to envision a day when I wouldn't have to wrestle with Colter over his urge to run to the horizon and beyond, to run to wherever the scent was. I knew Jarrett was right, but I just couldn't picture it, and so I quickly put the notion out of mind. Maybe in another seven or eight years I'd consider it again. In the meantime, I could no more imagine a slowing-down Colter than I could a slow-motion bolt of lightning in the night sky.

I shook Jarrett's hand. He smiled, but already seemed preoccupied. Quailsong drifted from the bird pens. Other dogs were barking, awaiting their turns. The day was warming.

Utter, utter freedom. Colter and I headed back west.

Seven

THE SPRUCE GROUSE aren't rare up here in the mountains yet — not the way sage grouse are, out on the plains — but they seem so vulnerable. I worry that someday soon we may know them only from photos and history books and old tales. It's not fair to say that spruce grouse are unwitting; fairer, perhaps, to say that the world has changed so quickly for them.

It's hard to get spruce grouse to fly wild. Usually they simply hop up in a branch and look down at you. This drives the dogs, especially the pointing dogs, nuts. And if, as my friend Tim and I sometimes do, you toss sticks up into the branches, trying to get the bird to make a good wild flush, the bird usually just hops over to another branch with a halfhearted little flutter. You can't shoot something like that. You just have to walk away.

Occasionally — rarely — I'll get a good enough

flush, under a good point, that I *can* shoot: and then, just as rarely, I'll hit the bird.

But a hunter or shooter who has no qualms about shooting them out of trees, or at the side of the road, can fill his or her limit easily, if only he or she can find the spruce grouse in the first place. The birds stand by obligingly. Often I'll find the residue of such an encounter: a bright, empty shotgun shell on the side of the road, a loose pile of feathers, and a carcass with the breast torn hastily out, leaving behind the wing and leg meat. Such scenes suggest to me that the only thing that will save the spruce grouse ultimately will be to preserve wild forests that can only be entered on foot. Then the spruce grouse might have a chance.

Although I think spruce grouse are the best-tasting of the three grouse found in the forests, all are delicious. I usually take only one or two per year, and watch the others flutter away unharmed, usually unshot at. I try to believe that as long as I let them go, the spruce grouse will still be around, as if the other huge forces of the world — development, habitat destruction and fragmentation by roadbuilding — are not gnawing away at them yearly.

There is this one particular covert I like to hunt, up on a forested plateau above the gravelly wash of a floodplain (the rubbly, well-drained leavings of glaciers a perfect seedbed for stands of aspen and cottonwood, with their breathtaking autumn colors); and almost always, in one tree there, I encounter one very large spruce grouse.

I never shoot at that bird. And I often take friends who have never seen a spruce grouse to see it.

After five years of leading such tours, it has occurred to me that perhaps it is not the same bird each year. (How could it be? Most grouse don't live beyond the ripe old age of two.) I imagine instead that the forest, the landscape, is producing and sculpting a new bird for that one spot year after year: and that all living things are but manifestations of the folds of landscape, and the coils and stirrings and vectors of energy within that place and time; and that spot, and that one tree, desires to have a plump spruce grouse sitting in it, one year after another.

If you can believe such a thing — if you can even consider such a thing — then you can understand that my traveling to that tree each year to see the new bird of the year has become a kind of pilgrimage, a voyage.

This season I got one of my two spruce grouse by accident, or fate. Elizabeth was driving home near dusk when she spotted a grouse lying in the dusty road. She stopped, examined it, found it to be still warm and limp, fully feathered, so she put it in the grocery bag and continued on home. In a high bird year a grouse or two will often flush wild from the roadside alders and be struck by a truck or car.

But what was curious was that I had driven down the road not five minutes ahead of Elizabeth; and the dead grouse had not been there then. I knew I hadn't hit a bird, but once I got home, I didn't hear any other cars go down the road.

I admired the beautiful black and cream and gold

plumage, the red eye patch, and then hung the bird in the shade of the back porch to age.

When I sat down to clean it a few days later, I was surprised to find no broken bones. The trouble with roadkill is that often the small bones of birds are broken in so many places that it makes for uncomfortable eating. This bird, however, was perfect. I examined it again, and noticed now what I had overlooked earlier, in admiring the plumage: the eyes, which I had previously assumed to be shut in death, were instead missing; something had pecked them out.

A hawk, probably a goshawk, had caught and killed this grouse in the brief time between my truck and Elizabeth's. The hawk must have just settled in to the kill — resting for a short while, calming its wild heart and preening, and then taking the first tentative bites, pecking at the eyes — when Elizabeth's truck scared it away. Perhaps it flew to the high branches of a big larch and perched and waited, and watched.

Imagine the hawk's dismay at seeing the truck stop, and Elizabeth get out, pick up the grouse, then drive off with it!

What restitution can be made?

I'm sorry.

It was a delicious meal.

Eight

IN MID-OCTOBER, Colter and I went pheasant hunting again, with Tim and Maddie and our friend Todd. Late in the afternoon a crisp north wind rattled the yellow cottonwood leaves in front of a farmhouse as we walked along an irrigation levee across the road. Colter was sitting this one out, back at the truck — *benched* — because he broke wild on a flush and a missed shot. I think he was frustrated by my missing, but it didn't matter: he had to be reined back in. I'd found that whenever he slipped and messed up, sitting him out for a run was the worst punishment imaginable for him. He would come right back to his own perfect self on the next run.

So Tim and Todd and I were hunting along behind Maddie, and though it was beautiful beneath that blue sky, with the gold dog snuffling ahead of us in the gold grasses, I was feeling a little empty, a little lonely, without the thrashing wild brown man tearing up the countryside in front of me.

Jarrett warned me that the field was a big place — that there are infinite temptations for both a young dog and a young hunter; that if you, the hunter, let the dog's performance erode just a little, it could be the beginning of an ever-downward spiral back to a talented but erratic dog — perfect some days, mediocre on others. And Jarrett knew I was exactly the kind of owner at risk for that, the kind who was going to love his dog and find something positive about his performance no matter what he did.

So I was walking along, trying to be stern — we were still in full view of Colter, who was sitting up in the driver's seat with his nose pressed against the curve of the windshield — when Maddie kicked a rooster out on my left.

The bird bailed fast downslope, and almost in a trance, I made the shot, and for the only time in my life, before or since, I felt no jubilation at making it, but instead only a windy kind of silence. When I looked back at the truck where the little bomber-man was caged and heard his frantic, plaintive barking, I told Tim and Todd, "I feel like I'm being *unfaithful*."

We decided to cut short that run so we could spring Colter from his penance. He thrashed all around in the front seat when he saw us returning, ecstatic, knowing he was being given another chance — and knowing, I think, in his pure athlete's heart, that he would produce to perfection this time (even if his shooters didn't).

He grinned his big toothy grin and leapt from the truck like a rocket when we opened the door, running in mad circles and slashes, cutting divots in the dark earth and wheat stubble; grinning and yelping, he set off into the wind. We hunted up a steep canyon, a rose-choked draw, and Colter pointed a small flock of sharp-tails. But the birds were skittish, and flushed just out of range.

We watched them fly away, out over the horizon, then broke our guns and walked down the hill, back through the stubble-field, toward the road, toward the massive cottonwoods surrounding the little farmhouse. The afternoon wind was chilly, and the dry yellow leaves chattered like teeth. A light was on already inside the house, giving the premature appearance of evening. It was a neat homestead, like most of them in that wind-scoured country: bright red barns and outbuildings, bright white picket fences. In the old days — a hundred, two hundred, three hundred years ago — people from our valley used to cross over here in the early autumn to hunt buffalo. Now we were making the same trip to hunt a creature, the ring-necked pheasant, that was one-one-thousandth the size of a buffalo, and which didn't even exist here then. Still, it felt right, or like the echo of right, which may be as close as we can get, these days, to our ancestral identities — our old paths and boundaries.

We stopped on the last rise, admiring the scene below us. In the tall cottonwoods sat an enormous great horned owl. At first we thought he too was admiring, or observing, the farmhouse, but then we saw that his yellow eyes were fixed on a black cat skulking through the stubble.

And then we saw a bright rooster in the yard, on the other side of the picket fence, rustling among the yellow leaves, and that the cat was stalking that long-tailed rooster, even as the owl, with its eyes, was stalking the cat.

It was growing late. We veered away, to keep from interrupting things. We had time for one more hunt.

Nine

I AM SO ENRAPTURED with Colter that I have asked Tom and Nancy if they would breed his mother, Paggon, one last time, to the same male, his father — Kootenai Clay. I've become addicted to dogs. My heart has become inflamed, watching Colter. Most people spread the ages of their hunting dogs about five years apart, but I can't wait, don't want to wait — and I don't want to risk losing a litter out of Paggon, who is seven years old now, pushing eight.

So now I am driving fifteen miles up the valley almost every day, to go look at her new litter: trying to decide on *the* one. There are four males and four females, and Tom and Nancy have graciously allowed me the pick of the litter. I know that as inexperienced as I am I should choose a female, playing the odds that she might be more biddable, less hard-headed — but I am so in love with Colter — his eagerness to cover immense ground, his manic, dopey goofiness — his bodybuilder's physique, and his unique and developing mixture of recklessness and caution — that I'm afraid to try a female, that she might have too different a style. *I want a Colter clone,* or as close to it as I can get.

My four-year-old daughter Mary Katherine rides over there with me daily. Jarrett has said that in choosing a pup, it's good to notice which one pays close attention to your voice.

Gold sunlight pours in through the loft window, illuminating the tiny pups — six chocolates, two ticked (one male, one female) — and Mary Katherine crawling and rolling around squealing with them. I realize that I don't *want* to choose: I just want to keep coming here every day.

Tom is bemused but patient with my growing quandary: the more time I spend around the pups, the more I realize each one's qualities. "Look at Colter," he and Nancy remind me. "The runt of the litter, and look how he turned out."

It should be easy. Four males to choose from, right? Three browns, one ticked. Since I want a Colter clone, that means a brown one: one of three. But the way they wriggle and lick and chew on you — each reacting differently to the other, too — how can you choose? I'm tempted to just shut my eyes and point into the mass of writhing brown.

"You can't tell anything about them at this age, anyway," Tom says. "It's what you put into them that counts."

Nancy has one in each hand; they're giving her kisses. "Isn't it amazing how their breath smells like coffee grounds?" she says.

Mary Katherine decides she wants "that little spotted female" — a beautiful, elegant, trim ticked pup. Over and over she insists she's in love with that one — and knowing of the prescience of children, I start to waver. Driving home, I begin to reconsider: a little female *would* be nice, wouldn't it? I wonder if anyone else dreams as frequently as I do of being afield with their dog, and finding birds — swinging on the birds then, in the dream, and firing, and always (this is the great thing about dreams), always connecting?

I have that dream — always a different covert, usually grouse, but sometimes pheasant or quail — fifteen, twenty times a year.

My freezer should be as full as my dreams.

Tom came up here twenty years ago, after he retired from the rodeo — he was a bronc rider — and decided to live off the land. He had an old ticked shorthair named Nuthin' who was, to hear Tom talk about him — and I've never heard Tom exaggerate — about the best dog there ever was. The first couple of years I was in the valley, in the autumn I'd often see Tom walking down a dirt road late in the afternoon, dressed in his buckskins, carrying a big old goshawk on one arm, with Nuthin' working the cover ahead of them. No one knows why, but dogs and cats live an extraordinarily long time in this valley, and Nuthin' was seventeen before he started to fade — his eyes and ears, his hips, everything of consequence.

Tom went down to the vet for pain pills but told us that when he ran out of them that was going to be Nuthin's last day, and I remember the incredibly sad uneasiness I felt as I hiked through the valley then, trying to remember which day it was: if Tom had four pills left, or three, or if it was down to two, or if today was the last day.

Trying to stay away from that end of the valley, to avoid hearing the shot.

Paggon begins to think that Mary Katherine's her ninth pup, she's spent so much time crawling around with them. There is one sweet brown boy I call Superman, for the big white-ticked vee on his chest, like the symbol beneath the cartoon character's cape, who just melts in my arms: rolls over on his back and stretches his neck out to be scratched; but there is also the ticked male, tiny, whom Tom and Nancy call "Point," because already he is pointing — incredibly focused with precise, sneaking steps — the grouse wing tied to the end of a bamboo pole. This dog is, for the moment, clearly establishing itself as the birdiest pup, but when I scoop him up to love him, he tenses, then wriggles to get free — wanting nothing but to hunt.

Do I go with the lover, or the machine? Or the little spotted female?

Point has his tail docked extra long, to leave a little tip of white on it at the end; he'll be more visible in the valley's dark coverts. It'll be a little longer than most shorthairs' stubs. I am attracted to this notion of otherness, roughness, unorthodoxy. This valley's not like any other place in the world, dark and mysterious and ragged, and I like the idea of a dog like that.

Tom and Nancy have moved the pups outdoors, to be near them while they work on the hides. The pups nap during the heat of the day in an old tent strung over a rope tied between two trees: a pup tent. They wrestle and fight for possession of their sole toy, a coyote tail. Tom and Nancy look up from their work often, keeping a close eye on them to be sure they don't wander off into the forest and get snagged by a hawk or coyote. They're not much larger than the grouse we'll be putting them on five or six months from now. Their little piles of poop look remarkably like those of their quarry.

I feel I have to go with my heart: the solid brown lovable Colter-clone, Superman. And yet, I also have to go with my daughters' choice, a speckled pup — though because of my fondness for male pointers, I'll choose a speckled male instead of a female; and of these, Point is clearly the pick of the litter.

All my life I have had this problem of loving too much, of wanting too much — a passion so intense as to approach gluttony. It bothers me, and I have been trying for a long time to cut back on both the volume and magnitude of my desires. Sometimes it makes me feel a little ashamed that neither my heart nor my appetite, even now, near forty, knows any restraint. Perhaps it is this way for Colter when he runs too far or too hard, when he allows himself to be drawn too enthusiastically, even recklessly, toward the scent cone of the huddled birds and runs over the top of them, busting them wild and without point.

Even on the days when I am able to relax and hold back on my desires, or my joy, there is always the awareness that it is a conscious, "unnatural" act, and in some ways I am more unnerved by that artificiality than I am by the problem of wanting to go after the world hog-wild, of almost never, ever being satisfied.

I know it's a sin, that gluttony — a handicap, like some injury to the soul. I just don't know what to do about it. But why not two dogs, I ask myself?

Or rather, two more, for a total of five. What's the difference, really, between four and five? Colter was down in Texas, at Jarrett's. Homer and Ann, my sweet hounds, were getting old. There seemed to be a nice symmetry to things the two old female hounds (who had never been any trouble, and who had in fact helped balance and take care of one another; friends, twin sisters) counterbalanced eleven years later by two young male pointers, Point and Superman — with the great Colter anchoring the five dogs, in between the two sets of twins. *Yes,* my blood, or the valley, or both, whispered.

I kept the idea secret for another week, not daring to utter it yet to Elizabeth: until one day she herself uttered it. There was no way to choose between the two. And it *was* Paggon's last litter.

"A fine idea," I said, my eyes smarting with joy tears. "Yes. A good idea. All right. O.K. Good idea."

Ten

W E DON'T KILL A LOT of birds because I'm not a very good shot, but we end up with enough simply by dint of being out in the field so often, and so long.

A thing that speaks to me of autumn even more than the hunting and shooting (or not shooting) of the birds, and even more than the changing colors of the leaves and the first hard frost at night, is the waning-dusk ritual of plucking the bird we've gotten that day. (Needless to say, it doesn't happen every day; that's one of the things that makes it special.)

I'll sit on the porch steps looking out at the woods to the west, plucking the soft feathers from the still-warm breast, and plucking them from the back, the legs, the wings — everywhere. You can still eat the skin of birds from western Montana, from the forest, though the government advises avoiding the skin of birds from eastern Montana, so saturated with the residues of herbicide and pesticide.

Nonetheless, I pluck them all, as sacrament — to merely jerk the skin free and pull out the breast seems disrespectful — and I cook them, eastern and western both, with the skin still on, to help keep in the juices and the taste of the body; though with the prairie birds, it's true, I don't eat the skin, but feed it to the dogs after cooking it, especially to old Homer and Ann, who already are pushing eighty, and who no longer need to worry about such things.

I save the ornate tail feathers (whether grouse, pheasant, or Hun) and put the rest of the feathers and entrails in a bag, which I dump out in the woods, to return to other animals, and to the soil, to return to the sky.

The crops, however, I examine closely, to see what each bird has been feeding upon.

Clover. Kinnickkinnick. Snowberries. Wheat. Barley. Crickets. Grasshoppers. Fir needles. Huckleberries. Rose hips.

The crops filled with snowberries are breathtaking, looking like a clump of pearls, and nearly as rare; it's always a thrill to open a crop and see nothing but beautiful white berries.

Usually in these woods, though, in the autumn, the crops are bulging with bright red kinnickkinnick berries, and the bright green leaves from the same bush.

Tom and Nancy save the crop from each bird they kill and set it on the windowsill to dry translucent in the sunlight — a globe, a ball, filled with Christmas colors, perfect red and green; and then in December they hang these as ornaments on their tree.

For the eastern birds, the crops are almost always

filled with wheat. It's a strange and exotic sight, to be sitting there on my porch steps way deep in the rainy backwoods of northwest Montana, and to find small handfuls of wheat in the crop of the bird I'm holding. As if, for a moment, I've returned to that foreign, distant land — not just in memory, but in reality, because look, there is the proof in my hand.

Colter will usually be running restless laps around me while I pluck the birds, excited by the scent again, and perhaps hoping that, against all odds — like producing a rabbit from beneath a handkerchief — another bird, a live bird, will somehow erupt from out of the scent of all those swirling feathers. He comes up on the porch, snuffles his nose into the feather bag (loose feathers stick to his nose), then nuzzles his bony head in under my elbow, trying to be petted while I work.

I don't save the crops. I toss them out into the yard, perhaps in the way the old pagans used to hurl entrails at the ground, in an attempt to forecast the future. From a sitting position, I fling them out across the gravel driveway, across the stone wall, and into the yard, where the native fruits from the grouse — snowberries, wild rose, kinnickkinnick — will take root, and grow, in wandering, random patterns.

And even more amazingly, in subsequent years, grouse and other birds will sometimes venture into the yard to feed on the fruit of these crop-birthed plants: strutting around in the yard, feeding on berries grown from the plants that their ancestors had been feeding upon when they died. Pecking around in the yard, pecking at those snowberries, those kinnickkinnick berries, it's as if reading the wandering words of curling sentences, little stories, out there in the yard.

At the edge of my gravel driveway, up against the rock wall, stands the only patch of wheat in northwestern Montana. One of the crops from an eastern bird must not have made it all the way into the yard, and the yard would have been too wet and shady for wheat to grow, anyway: but in the artificial, well-drained habitat of the gravel driveway the wheat has germinated and prospered.

It's just a little patch, not much larger than a wheelbarrow. But you'd have to drive three hundred miles to find any other wheat in Montana. And I like looking at it, and knowing how it got there.

We are farmers of a kind, Colter and I.

Eleven

IN LATE JULY I went over to Tom and Nancy's, six weeks after the pups were born, to get them and bring them home. Nancy cried as I was leaving. For forty-two days she had had puppies in her arms, puppies in her hands, puppies all over her, for all hours of the day and night. Forty-two days and nights of playing with them, petting them, loving them: imparting a sweetness to them with her incessant handling and petting of them as a potter might work a piece of clay. She was that way with Colter and his littermates, three years earlier, and it was one of the reasons I wanted a Colter-clone. My last chance, it seemed, at such an animal.

The pups whined and cried all the way home. So tiny: arriving home I got out of the truck, holding one round-bellied pup in each hand, as I had once carried Homer and Ann when I found them by the road.

I wondered if these pups would send my life lurching into some new gear as Homer and Ann had. And Colter. The thought terrified me. Everything I needed, I already had. I just loved dogs, was all.

I imagined all of the future hunts we would have, the magical future I was literally holding in my hands.

It grew hot in the next few days; August came like a wall of fire. Dogs, so susceptible to heat, began to crack under the pressure, falling ill to various maladies, to previously unrevealed stresses that might never have been noticed if the temperatures had stayed in the nineties.

When the temperature crossed over the hundred-degree mark, the vet's office was full day and night with both dogs and cats. And out in the woods, the lions and wolves and bears and coyotes were stirring — coming into the yards to pound on the domestic animals. Human tempers rose as well. The moon waxed.

Tim and Joanne's sweet Maddie fell ill — throwing up, then retching. Doug, the vet, did exploratory surgery on her and found that her intestines had somehow decomposed; though she was only seven, and should have been in her prime, there was just nothing left, and only twenty-four hours after she had started vomiting she had to be put to sleep. Tim had to keep guiding on the river; he couldn't let his clients down. Earlier in the summer he and Joanne had bought a new pup, Jessie — also a female golden retriever — in the hopes that Maddie would help train the pup.

Now, with hunting season three weeks away, Maddie was gone, and it was like an interruption of grace.

*　　*　　*

One day it hit 103 degrees. Friends had come to visit with their children and we decided to go down to bathe in the cool river below the falls, in the shallows.

The pups, Point and Superman, had commandeered the prime spot under the porch, by virtue of their incessant badgering and ear-biting and tail-nipping. Homer had retreated to the back porch, where, the instant that door was opened, she scooted inside to spend the rest of the afternoon sleeping on the cool tiles of the utility room.

Ann would never relinquish daylight. At the age of eleven she was starting to slow down, but she was always out at dawn, and then back at dusk: never traveling far, only patrolling the perimeter of the yard. The trails through those woods within sight of the house were trampled clean in a spidery, wandering skein that spoke of her passage: a trail as well worn as if carved by man and his machines, rather than the soft padded feet and wandering curiosity of a hound.

She had never slept beneath a truck or car before, but she had never been eleven in August before, had never seen it hit 103 degrees in Montana before — had never been plagued by twin devil-pups before.

It must have been cool, in the gravel beneath the shade of the truck.

I got in our guests' van to show them the way to the river. They waved to Elizabeth to lead the way. As she backed up, I heard an awful yelping. I thought it was one of the pups. I leapt out of the van and saw Ann thrashing and flapping in the gravel. Elizabeth had bought big new snow tires that week, to beat the autumn rush, and the tires had rolled over Ann and dragged her a ways. She tried to stand, but kept falling down again. I'd never heard her yelp in pain like that, not in eleven years.

I hurried over to her. She finally managed to stand, but then fell again. I picked her up and she bit me hard — clamped down and wouldn't, couldn't, let go — I felt her teeth pass through the palm of my hand and through my thumbnail, felt her upper and lower teeth tear all the way through the meat of my hand with a single crush. Hard to believe this little beagle-sized hound could bite so hard. I was crying, holding her, not saying anything as the blood from my hand began to trickle from her mouth. I tried to absorb, through my hand, some of her pain. Her eyes were squeezed shut. With my free hand I petted her, and with her eyes still shut and teeth still latched through my hand, she wagged her tail.

I put her on the front seat of the truck, told everyone good-bye, and raced for the vet. It was a Saturday. I drove fast, petting her, with her head on my lap all the way. Her breathing was slow and shallow and her eyes steady and unblinking. She had always been such a strong little dog — glorying in her strength. Though she only weighed forty pounds, she pulled us on skis, and she fought with the coyotes when they came in the yard. The little bear, the little bull, we called her. Long, long eyelashes, like a queen. Almost always, a little smile.

Elizabeth had called ahead, so that Doug was waiting for me. Doug checked Ann's pulse, temperature, and eyes before running an x-ray. She had a broken hip bone, but that seemed to be it. It was all I could do to keep from crying with the weakness of relief — the miracle of it. We turned her over to check the other side and I noticed something strange about Ann's rib cage — as if two or three ribs were missing.

"Yes," said Doug, "something's different there."

He ran a scan of some kind; I don't even remember what it was. I don't even remember what it showed; only that she was messed up inside.

Doug said my best bet was to drive her five hours to Pullman, Washington, where they could operate on her Monday. He could try the operation but they had better equipment and her chances were better there.

I was just wearing shorts, a t-shirt, sandals. I had brought no money. Doug loaned me two hundred dollars and I drove west. Doug poured some water for her, which she sipped, and wagged her tail again; she seemed, for a moment, like her old self.

Driving to Pullman, it was like I was a young man again, and she was a puppy: all the miles we'd traveled, all around the country. She had led me so many places — swimming in Mississippi lakes in the glinting sun, treeing squirrels in Central Park, chasing armadillos in Texas, and finally, the mountains in Montana — and she died shortly after we crossed over the Idaho line. She grew restless, uneasy, tried to shift around, then looked up at me one last time with troubled eyes, almost guilty, then dipped her head, and was still.

I grieved for a long time — the rest of the summer. I dug a deep hole for her in the yard, within sight of the front door, so she could continue to keep watch over us as she always had, and so she would not feel turned out or turned away, even in death.

Poor Homer! Her twin — the roadside sister, the other half of the magic, now alone — and in that solitude, does she possess more magic, or less? I've heard it said that when one dog of a pair dies you're supposed to show the other dog the body so that it can grieve too — but I did not have the strength, the courage, to do that to Homer. I hated my weakness, my softness, but I couldn't.

The next day Homer went to the spot where Ann had been crushed and sniffed at that spot, then lay down there and waited for a little while. And in subsequent days, she stood on the porch looking and watching and waiting — and watching me expectantly, as if depending on me to find Ann, and return her.

I buried her like a pagan. I put deer bones in with her, for her journey; a blanket, for warmth; flowers, cedar fronds, stones from places we'd been, grouse feathers, a tidbit of raw venison hamburger, and a swatch of my own hair. A headstone, a footstone. I planted an aspen tree above the headstone, to give her shade, and to someday provide leaf-music in the breeze.

It took a long time before I was worth a damn again. How to measure the eleven years of magic she brought to us? How, now, to say thank you? Too late, as usual, for these sorts of things.

Twelve

For a month after Ann died, I was paralyzed, unable to read or write, numb to the beauty of autumn. But I also felt an obligation to Colter, to his young heart and burning eyes.

My old truck wouldn't make it through the winter. Early one afternoon Colter and I drove down to Missoula, where I traded the old truck for one that's even older, but in better condition.

Then we headed farther south and east, toward Dillon, where I'd heard there's a huge ranch where the public is allowed to hunt for sage grouse.

We arrived in Dillon well after midnight. There was a rodeo in town the next day, so all the hotels were filled. I spread my sleeping bag in the back of the truck. It was a cold night — twinkling stars, and a serious frost forming — and I tried to show Colter how to get in the sleeping bag with me, but this was a thing that was definitely not in his blood, and so he spent the night draped across my knees on the outside, shivering but never whining — getting up and pacing around in the night, teeth chattering, waiting for morning, until settling his bony frame back down across my knees again, where he shivered so hard that the back of the truck rocked. A Texan, and a short-haired pointer! What were we doing this far north?

The sun's slant, early into September, still had enough bite to burn the frost off quickly the next day. We drove out into the country, found the vast ranch, parked on the side of the road, and I waited for a few minutes, savoring the blue sky, and freedom, and the health and vigor of my dog, and the scent of sage. A distant line of willows snaked through the distant prairie, beyond which lay the foothills. Colter was raring to go but I wanted to sit a moment longer, soaking in the autumn, and this new place, new pursuit.

A truck passed by with a dead moose in the back that looked as large as an elephant. Archery season. It took a while after the truck and moose were gone, for the notion of birds, not large mammals, to fill my blood again. In this way Colter will always be the master, and I the student. Birds are always in his blood.

I made sure I had everything in my vest: shells, pocketknife, water, lunch. I unloaded Colter and closed up the truck and and we set off. I have complete confidence in his nose and knew that if there was a sage grouse within our range — roughly twenty miles today, with him covering easily five times that distance — we would find it, and I would shoot at it, a one-in-five chance I might hit it.

Some days I'll go three-for-three, or three-for-four, or four-for-six, but there are longer stretches where I'm oh-for-twelve, or one-for-twenty-five. It averages out to about one-in-ten; and Colter, bless his wild heart, knows it, and does not back off a bit for knowing it. If anything, he pushes on harder than ever, and I think that it is so noble, for him to do this: to continue to hunt so hard for such a lousy shot.

We pushed out onto the prairie: my first steps of any consequence, of *doing* anything, since Ann died. All of the old clichés of rebirth, or healing, are so time-tested and maddeningly true. On that bright morning after traveling far through the night in a new-old truck and stepping out into a new place with my pal, my hunting partner, I felt like I was emerging blinking from a chrysalis. It was not reawakened emotion I felt — joy, regret, nostalgia, sorrow — but rather a return of the senses after a long numbness and confusion.

One would have thought joy, or happiness, or pleasure, would have been a component of this awakening. But it was nothing so complex as that. It was simply a clearer notion of scent and sound and vision; greater tactility. The edges of things seemed to have a sharpness they had not possessed the day before, or the day before that.

We launched ourselves into the wind, into the vastness of the country before us, making our way through hard-grazed stubble toward the winding green corridor of a creek, and the sage of the foothills beyond. The young dog was happy simply to run, casting perfectly, casting hugely, and it relaxed my heart as I watched the grace and ease of his long legs, and saw his continuous joy, uninterrupted by even the shadow of a passing, fleeting, negative thought.

Newborn, but older, I followed him, ever conscious of my responsibility to participate in his joy. He needed me.

It was hot. We struck the willows and he crossed the creek in a Herculean bound — easily fifteen feet — and I waded it to join him. We traveled upstream through tall grass and willows. He caught scent and moved in tight to a clump of willows, and went on point, though it was a tentative point, and with a bit of a hunched back.

I've seen him staunch on birds a thousand times, and he has never, ever, been wrong: not once, even as a puppy, has his body betrayed him. When his stub tail stops twitching — when it locks — you can be sure that the bird is there. Not the scent of where the bird was just a moment ago, but the bird itself, at this moment: the scent picture of the hidden bird painting itself, feather by feather, line by line, across his palate.

He wasn't staunch here: not at full point. But such was my grogginess from the month of grief that I wanted to force things — to force my dog to learn some restraint even as I, at the age of forty, have been unable to learn it.

"Whoa," I told him — he *whoaed* — and I kicked at the brush, wondering what would emerge. *Nothing.* "All right," I told Colter, "get that bird up."

He crept in, just as he's supposed to — I was so proud I could have burst — and I urged him on.

He caught sight of his unfamiliar quarry, and lunged.

It's a porcupine, and I mean to tell you, a big one. Colter yelped, backed away, and then, furious, attacked it again and again — two, three more savage bites. Colter was still attacking as I waded in and pulled him off the beast. Blood everywhere. An ivory pincushion obscured the face of my dog. He yelped with pain as he tried to spit out the quills lodged in the roof of his mouth. Every time he barked or panted or yelped he stabbed himself again with his mouthful of daggers. No quills in the eyes, thank God, but all around them, so that he looked as if he was wearing a clown's mask.

Like a rookie, an amateur, a sleepwalker, I was not carrying hemostats. I hadn't even brought any on the trip with me. Perhaps I do not deserve this dog. I did have some scissors in the truck, so we headed straight back to it. You can't just pull porcupine quills; you've got to snip the ends off to deflate them, *then* snatch them out. Otherwise it's like trying to pull fish hooks.

It was a Sunday, of course, and we were damn near a hundred miles from a vet.

I asked Colter to heel, so I could pet him and soothe him as he trotted alongside me, but he wouldn't have any of it: as ever, he raced out ahead of me, hunting hard, casting.

We spent only two and a half hours pulling quills, though it seemed like days. I stopped counting near two hundred. Bits and pieces of clipped quills were scattered all over the road, all over the tailgate/operating table. Quite understandably, Colter didn't want me tugging on those quills. As I snipped and then gripped each one, saliva-slippery, with the needlenose pliers, and jerked, he squalled and yelped, lunged and twisted and writhed. He was far too strong for me to restrain and pluck at the same time, so I had to truss and halter and bind him, stanchioned every which way, but still he twisted and rolled like a pretzel, winding himself (and me with him, hunched over him) into a corkscrew and then back out again, so that the scene there under the big sky and the lone prairie, unobserved by the eye of man, was like that of an anaconda wrestling with a hapless deer.

I don't know how it ever ended, but it finally did. I offered Colter some water, but he didn't want it. I tried to entice him to kennel up, but no dice: he skittered away, dancing out into the field, anxious to resume hunting.

To feel the world again, to taste it, to see it, drinking it in, like gulps of air. We jumped a lot of deer — whitetails — out of the willows, but Colter's learned not to chase them. I was tempted to not hunt anymore, worried he'd go after another porcupine, demanding a rematch — his heart is larger than his considerable brain — but I knew that we had to get back out there and try.

We made it over to the foothills unscathed, and we broke even: we found nothing, but nothing found us. There was one tense moment when, moving hard through the sage, zigging and zagging, Colter sprung right over the top of a snarling badger. I was right behind Colter, and as the badger charged out of his burrow, all I could see were teeth — but I veered hard left, to the north, while the badger's rush carried him south. For a long time afterward the image of the badger's teeth and rank musculature stuck in my mind, and I began to wonder if there was some hellish gauntlet, some series of challenges through which all dogs and hunters must pass to reach the land of sage grouse.

Whatever the price to be paid, it felt good to be free again.

Bird dogs are crazy. Hunting, they charge out and seize the world with great boilermaker hearts, attempting to bend and alter the world, it seems, to their desire. Who can say what they're thinking? When they're off duty, they nap, as Colter does, resplendent and brown, in the light outside my writing cabin, in his little nest of grass at the edge of the marsh, eyes shut in bliss, a slight snore rumbling from his bony frame. He leads me out to my writing cabin each morning and, if it is not raining, sleeps there until I come out in the afternoon. Over a few short years the weight of his sleeping body has pressed the earth down in that one spot, sculpted it to his shape: muscular shoulders, deep chest, tiny waist, gaunt hips — head laid straight out, neck stretched, as if on point, even in his sleep.

In his absence I have examined the mold he has left in the earth, the ground packed hard as fired clay. I have run my hands over the inverted cast of those deep shoulders and bony hips and I lie down in it, to get a dog's-eye view of the world. A wall of grass rises like a corn field against the blue sky. It doesn't seem like a bad way, or place, to spend a life.

A dog's heart is at least as knowledgeable as his nose, and I wonder, as I write, how much he picks up of my rhythms, my emotions from sentence to sentence. I wonder if he senses, through the thin closed door, the moods of whatever I'm working on that day — or if he just sleeps.

When I come out of the cabin in the afternoon, he yawns, stretches, pulls his leggy self back up from that place of pleasure, and, still a little groggy, follows me back to the house. There are a series of steppingstones we use to keep our feet dry in wet weather, and our steps mimic each other's, stone for stone, as if we are crossing a stream in single-file unison. Somewhere along the way he will pick up a stick or a branch and move in closer and tap me against the back of my knees with it, lightly, as if urging me along like a goat herd, because he knows that once I am up at the house then I am in a far readier position to get my gun and vest and go out to the truck and call for him to kennel up: not that the words ever need to be spoken; he leaps into the front seat the second the door is opened.

I never go out to my cabin as eagerly as he leaps into the truck, which, I suppose, is why dogs are dogs and humans are, most days, humans. I never leap into my cabin. I trudge, often needing a goat herd in both directions.

In the field with him, in the autumn, though, as we move through the light and shadows, I can hear, somedays dimly but other days as if with a shouted roar, some of the silent fury and joy passing through his blood as he runs — and I can almost feel it in my own blood.

*　　*　　*

We pushed on up a dry wash, deeper into sage country now. The sage made a rich smell as Colter smashed through it and I crushed it with my boots. I was anxious to know what the meat of a bird that feeds on sage tastes like.

Colter followed some mystery scent upslope for a minute or two, but it turned out to be a cottontail; he flushed it, then veered away, satisfied, it seems, to have merely disrupted the rabbit's rhythms.

We pounded those hot hills for an hour, finding no birds, but there were beautiful flecks of turquoise underfoot, some of which I pocketed to take back home to the rain forest. I stopped often and poured water into my cupped hand for Colter to drink, but as usual, he was too jazzed to drink. He drank all the water in his bowl in the hotel room that night, and then, at four A.M., as I was trying to sleep, he got up and lapped all the water out of the toilet bowl, too — drinking steadily for about fifteen minutes, the lapping sound amplified by the acoustics of the porcelain curve, and his dog tags jingling mightily — but that day, under the broad sun, he didn't have time for water.

After a long while, we gave up on the hills and turned back down toward the flats. There were some abandoned outbuildings a mile or two distant, shimmering blue and gray in the haze, and I pointed Colter toward them without a word. I've heard people say that their dog would "hunt his heart out" for them, but the way things are between me and Colter, I think each of us would hunt our hearts out for ourselves, and in that respect we are a good match. I wouldn't mind hunting to the horizon on any day, every day, and I know that Colter feels the same. In this respect we're not master and dog, but partners. He would choose the birds over me. He can't help it.

Softer than he, I would choose him over the birds. It's why I trail him.

He reached the creek, dived in — swam in circles, grinning. The autumn light ignited his eyes like gold candles; he grinned like a kid as he swam in circles in the deep hole. Then he hauled himself out, ribs tight against his slickened skin, shook once in his goofy, rattling, disjointed hound way — the back half shaking totally independent of the front half — and then he was off again, galloping, fluidity and grace, and for a moment, just a moment, I caught a whiff, an inkling, of how it must feel to be running cool and damp through all that hot dry air, and to be that young and strong.

He made game near the old homestead: snuffled about, darted this way and that — seemingly crazed and frantic, I was sure, to an outsider — a million pieces of data igniting in his brainpan, blossoming to incandescence. There was grouse scat and downy feathers everywhere; he made his read, his decision, and dashed off toward the creek, and I followed, but after three or four hours of walking, I was not ready, I was not alert — I was just out walking, rather than hunting — and when he went on point and I moved toward him, the birds, too many of them, flushed out ahead of me, and I took too much time choosing one. I fired twice at a distant going-away bird, missing both times.

Colter held staunch. The flock set back down not

too far away, and we moved off toward them. He stopped after a few steps, pointed again — a single was still hidden — and when this one got up, no excuses, no one could ask for more, I missed by a mile, shooting so far behind the bird that to even a casual observer it would have seemed that I was *trying* to miss the bird.

And at the sound of my shots, the rest of the flock got up once more, and this time they flew a long, long way — flying south, until we could no longer see them.

We traveled for a long time toward the horizon over which they disappeared but we did not find them again.

The thing about grief or sadness — even if it is over such a seemingly "lesser" creature as a dog — is that it takes away your strength and your endurance, as any injury does. Later that afternoon the sadness hit me, as did the loneliness of the country, and the paucity of sage grouse. So we fled north, to look for sharp-tails, and to draw closer to home and family, as if I had overextended, getting so far from home, not yet having regained my heart's stamina.

We stopped at a chain motel in the state capital. It was raining like hell, sleeting, with thunder and lightning too. We walked down the hallway — it was after midnight — like tired businessmen, and I set the alarm for dawn.

The next morning, as the sun was rising clear, we were up and driving north along the Rocky Mountain front: the towering reef of mountains leaping above us, as if we were traveling beneath a frozen wave of stone, as if we were the only things moving, the only signs of life, on that sea.

A distinctive mesa rose out of the prairie. There was a brightly painted farmhouse at the foot of the mesa shrouded by a dense grove of fruit trees. I turned and drove slowly down the gravel lane toward the house. Antelope watched us pass. Fierce rooster pheasants ran cackling down the drive, running for the house, before darting beneath the fruit trees. Red and golden apples littered the green grass.

A window was open upstairs with curtains blowing in the breeze. I stopped, got out, and knocked on the door.

A woman appeared at the door. She was dressed nicely, as if on her way to some important meeting, yet a meeting among friends.

"You must be a bird hunter. You can probably find some birds over by that silo," she said, pointing across the road. "There's about three hundred acres over there."

I thanked her and asked, "What about those pheasants, later in the year — can they be hunted?"

"No," she said sweetly, but with a bit of her autumn generosity thinning, "we like to keep those around to look at."

I thanked her again and drove off toward the silo. I parked before the rolling field of land left fallow in the Conservation Reserve Program, for erosion control and wildlife habitat — and again couldn't shake the feeling, nor did I wish to, that everyone in the world had vanished except Colter and me. And that there might possibly be sharp-tails out in that sea of grass.

We launched ourselves into the grass, quartering the wind. We aimed to patrol the perimeters like a combine, then clean up in the middle. Colter would eat the half-section like a giant threshing machine.

He went straight to the first covey, as was his habit, but he bumped them, or rather, they got up wild. I shot anyway, so excited was I to hear them chuckling and to see the white undersides of their wings flapping like banners against the blue sky. They were flying high and fast and away, and I shot twice, missing of course, and Colter ran after them barking, and bumped more. I shot at those, and missed them, too. Colter became unglued — I shot when he did not make a staunch point; I changed the rules on him — and he accelerated, running after those birds and howling. I wondered if the kind lady in the farmhouse was watching — she could certainly hear the shooting, and Colter's barking.

How strange it must be for a dog to be taken out of the dark wet fungal shadows of grousedom and turned loose in a land that receives only a tenth as much rain. In the distance Colter bumped more birds, ran howling after them, and my confidence in him weakened; for a moment I felt like sitting down and weeping.

Instead I shouted, whistled, and waited. Colter came slinking back, knowing he'd done wrong, but, hey, it was only a *little* wrong! Chill out, Pop! He also has a trick of pretending to scent game right in my

vicinity — snuffling for a moment, feinting, darting —
so that for a moment I can't help but wonder if there's
a bird hidden right under my feet. Only once in maybe
a thousand such times has there actually been a bird,
but I fall for Colter's trick every time, and my anger
fades.

We settled in to the real hunt. Colter cast big, ran
big, for about ten minutes before making game again,
and making it with penance this time — moving forward with a strange combination of recklessness and
caution that was beautiful to see, especially in a dog so
desirous of running with the throttle wide open.

He drew as close as he possibly could — crept,
pointed — and then the birds must have skittered
away beneath some tunnel of grass, because he pussy-
footed forward again — being careful not to run up
over them, in his enthusiasm — and with my heart
beating about two hundred times a minute, I stepped
in to flank him . . . the birds got up, I shot one and it
tumbled, and like a pro Colter still held, until I released him. He bounded over to the bird, mouthed
it — sharp-tail blood, his first ever, the best-eating bird
there is, I'm told — and though he did not bring it all
the way to me on the retrieve, he came halfway, and I
reached down and took it from him and spent a long
time letting him know that he is just the most amazing
damn animal on the earth.

We repeated the process twice more that afternoon,
so that we had three of the beautiful birds in hand
when we headed back to the truck. They seem to bleed
more than other grouse, and there were drops of
bright red blood stark against their snowy chests, like

the red trim around the door of the white farmhouse of the lady who betrayed them, though it was not she who betrayed them of course, but Colter: or rather, if there were any betrayal, it was their own rank and delicious scent, which Colter's family has been pursuing for generations.

We sat on the roadside and drew the birds; I wouldn't pluck them there, but instead took them back to the rainy valley where I live, to show my family, as if returning with rare and interesting specimens from the deepest Congo. The crop of each bird was packed jam-tight with wheat seeds and crickets, so that it looked like some kind of strange quiche. One of the crickets was still moving, though sluggishly. I released it back into the wheat, but could tell that it was not going to make it.

There are robins up here in the north woods, not the lazy puff-breasted suburban lawn robins but gaunt, harrow-eyed, dive-bombing shadows that veer away with such suddenness that at first I think they are hawks — northern goshawks, their natural predator. The long shadow's distance of twilight, and half a second, one second, two seconds at most, is all that separates the robin from the goshawk: and in that moment I can see how the swerve of wings, plunge and plummet of escape, has been carved and sculpted by the pursuit.

Though I love to hunt with friends, these parallel, sometimes overlapping lines of grace, where shadow and object merge and become for some few moments indistinguishable, have come only when Colter and I have been alone in the field. I hate trying to capture these moments of grace with paper and pen — with drying ink on paper. It is like trying to drop a fleeing sharp-tail by throwing a pen at it, or an apple. They usually come on the second or third day of hunting. We've both made mistakes. Colter has misbehaved just enough, and then some, to show that he still has spirit, and that it is a partnership: that he is not a mule hitched to a harness. And I will have missed shots.

The moments come in big country. The visual imprint, visual palate, is gold wheat and brown dog, or brown bush and gold dog. The dog is ranging big and steady into the wind, head up, charging, in perfect casts uninstructed by any trainer, and dependent upon the terrain — and the hunter is also moving steadily forward into that wind — walking briskly. The dog has adjusted his casts to fit the hunter's steady progress.

There is nothing ahead of them but more country — no borders. Everything is behind them: everything. There are two lines of movement — the north-south stride of the hunter and the east-west stitching of the dog — both wanting only one thing, *a bird,* and wanting it so effortlessly and purely that they come the closest they will ever come to shared language. For several minutes they travel across the prairie like that, indistinguishable from one another in heart, in desire — until finally the scent cone is encountered, and the dog must leave that place in time, that striding harmony, and accelerate, super-charged, into his own greater, vaster capability to desire that bird . . . The hunter feels a charge of excitement as well, but much of it comes from the dog — the shadow, now — rather than the subject itself, *the bird* — and the hunter hurries forward to the completion of things, with the dog dashing and darting now, chasing the bird, running it, trying to capture it as a tornado perhaps tries (in flinging up trees and houses and people) to capture the soil.

These are the moments you remember, after the season is over: not whether you got the bird or not, but the approach: the process. The shadow of the thing, more than the thing itself. It's very strange, very beautiful.

Nothing but prairie, sky, wind. Nothing. You're walking along, striding big but tiny, keeping up with the heartworks of the dog, and he with yours. Sometimes you laugh out loud at how conjoined the two of you are.

We drove home, Colter curled up in the seat next to me. He seemed transformed by only two days and two hundred miles of running — as if he was no longer the hard-charging bruiser I came out here with, but some frail, bony little hound. With a dog that runs as hard and as long as Colter you can almost see the flesh melting as he runs — his ribs becoming sharper by the hour, until they are like a fine set of knives. As if his desire is eating him, and for that reason he is in greater peril from himself than is the bird.

He was wasted, emptied, finally. He curled up and tucked his nose beneath his flank, so that it was hard to tell where he began and ended, in his all-brownness. His bony little haunches were hunkered way up, folded sharply over his ribs like the wings of a bird nesting, its head tucked beneath its wings, roosting for the night: I saw in the curve of muscle and bone how his hind legs *are* wings, and how again his desire powers him into his own kind of swooping, slashing flight.

I think that in those moments, those perfect moments, when we are crossing the great fields like that, an observer looking down from a mile or two above — a bird's-eye view — would not believe that we were earthbound. I feel certain that that observer would see the two animals, man and dog, moving steadily across that prairie — one casting and weaving, the other continuing straight ahead — and would believe that they were two birds traveling in some graceful drift to some point, some location, known surely to their hearts.

Thirteen

IN AN EFFORT to improve myself, to try to become
worthy of this dog, I enrolled in a shooting school, so
that I might stand a better chance of rewarding Colter
with a dropped bird every now and then.

Like every hunter, I've occasionally wondered, after
having believed — viscerally — that a bird would fall,
only to see it keep on flying, fully feathered and un-
fazed, whether there wasn't something wrong with the
mechanics of the universe, rather than my shot, so perfect was my swing, my aim, my everything . . .

I finally cut through all that stuff though and accepted the truth that *I am a really bad shot.* Must we
resort to the cruel ambiguities of enumeration? Will
that satisfy you? Must I quantify my abasement?

I have shot a box of shells without hitting a quail
before.

Well, you might say, those little buggers are fast, and
everyone has his slumps.

No, I will say, gripping you by the shoulders, *listen*. I have shot a box of shells at *pheasants* before without hitting one.

I have made my peace with this condition; after much moral wrestling, I've succeeded in *not* defining my worth as a person by how well I shoot a shotgun.

I cannot explain this to Colter, however; and to be further truthful, my peace fades when I am with him, and he, through diligent effort and prodigious talent and desire-to-please — call it love — produces a bird, or birds, for me, and I fire and miss, again and again and again. The guilt, the regret returns.

None of us are worthy of our dogs. But we can try.

Six of us gathered at a beautiful hunting lodge in northern Montana on a glorious autumn day with fog like smoke among the soft humps of mountains — the larch needles red-gold, and the season's first snow, early October, already high above us in the roadless country beyond. Steve Schultz, our teacher, was as careful and gentle with us as, say, a social worker or family counselor; we understood that he truly wanted to help, and yet nowhere was there any feeling of pressure to change.

After breakfast we suited up and left the dining room with its magnificent views and trudged out into the blowing mist and fog. Steve delivered a safety talk, starting out with simple, vital gun etiquette, but concluding — effectively, I might add — with stories about friends and acquaintances that had been shot by students. For the entire course Steve would hold all of our shells in his vest, and would hand them to us one at a time, or insert them into the tube of the breached gun himself, as we stood there on the platform with him.

His cadence, his demeanor, reminded me of my own feelings on the opening day of bird season each fall. *All right,* I'll think, when I step out into the field for the first time, with Colter, in early September. *The whole field, the whole season, lies before me. The thing I've been waiting for is finally here.* You don't want to rush into it. You want to hang back for a moment and watch the world sweep past for a few beats. You want to notice everything.

Steve is a muscular man of medium height, in his early fifties. He's filled with aches and pains, shrapnel and scars, from Vietnam. He was once carried out in a black body bag, believed to be dead.

He asked us how far we think the pellets from a shotgun can travel and still be lethal. Our guesses clustered around the fifty-yard mark. One of us hazarded a guess of around a hundred yards. Steve told us that it's more like eight or nine hundred yards. We were silent for a moment, staring out at the vast autumn meadow beyond us, and the wall of blue trees — spruce and fire, with the gold coins of aspen leaves intermixed — beyond that.

Steve described people he's seen shot by shotguns: not in war, but while hunting. Crossing a fence, or swinging on a quail, or trudging out toward the goose decoys. It's like a hole opens up inside them, he said.

You're looking right at them and suddenly you can see daylight coming through them.

After another long pause — long enough for the image of that daylight to settle down somewhere inside us, as if we too had seen it, and will henceforth be ever vigilant against seeing it again — we stepped up to the shooting platform to begin. The lodge has several shooting stations placed all across the grounds, so that you can practice any kind of shooting you want: from a ridge looking down, straightaway, falling, rising, crossing . . . The pullers took turns crouching in the freezing drizzle with rapidly cooling cups of coffee and went down into a blind to wait the calls of *pull!* I could see a tiny thread of blue cigarette smoke rising from the blind below us, and I felt like some elite capitalist pig, playing up top while the yeoman labors below.

Anything for Colter.

Amazingly, we all shot about the same. Pretty piss-poor — about one- or two- or maybe three-for-twenty. (The three-for-twenties got bragged on and praised by us, though Steve just watched, *watched*. Personally I was thrilled, amazed, relieved that I nicked *anything* — a single pellet chipping the clay pigeon now and again. There's something so absolute and empty about the number zero.

"Good," Steve said, with true satisfaction, when the last of us had finished shooting, whiffing, poking, flailing. "You're all rifle shooters, not shotgunners." By which he meant that we were pointing and stabbing at the thing. And always, always shooting behind it, because it was moving.

He must love a challenge. It has gotten so easy for Steve to hit a clay pigeon — shooting left-handed, right-handed, upside-down — that the only serious challenge now was trying to get someone else to hit one. Trying to hit one no-handed, as it were — with both hands tied behind his back.

"Most of the birds you have killed in your life," he said, "have been by mistake." Pause. "That bird was in the wrong place at the wrong time." Pause. "An accident."

He proceeded to explain to us about the sight at the end of our barrels — the "miss-me bead." He demonstrated how, if you're looking at that bead, you're going to miss. He asked us to point a finger at a distant fence post and keep our eye on that fence post.

"Now," he said, "what happens when you look at the tip of your finger?"

The fence post disappeared, like magic. The bird flew away, in the time the eye spent refocusing on the tip of the finger, or the miss-me bead.

"So why do they put these beads on the ends of the barrel in the first place?" someone asked.

Steve pointed to the cap he was wearing, with the name "Federal" on it — the company he works for, the company that's helping sponsor our class. "So we can sell you lots of shotgun shells," he said.

Steve gave us an exercise, only one exercise, to do when we got back home: to practice mounting the gun in front of a mirror and looking down the rib, the spine, so that in the mirror all we can see is our eye, our one eye, at the other end of that same barrel. He said to do it slowly, smoothly, twenty-five times a day — not to build strength, but memory.

"It's the little things that get you," he said, meaning the tiny, initial inaccuracies that conspire to make you miss. If you take care of the basics, you will not miss. He guaranteed it — *you will not miss* — and we laughed nervously, not believing him, but understanding also that he was not conning us.

"Snug the gun up tight to the face," he said, showing us how to get a good mount. "Then look right down that rib. If you're wrong there — if you don't have the butt of the gun tight to your cheek, and if you're not sighting right down the rib — well, there's no telling where the shot string will go. You might be able to see the bird and it might appear to you that you're in the ballpark, that you've got a chance — but, depending on the distance, you'll probably be fifteen or twenty feet off — usually behind."

Steve showed us how to align the index finger of our left hand along the rib of the gun, so that when we swing the gun, we will literally be pointing that finger at the bird when we shoot. He asked how many of us had ever been driving down the road and seen a dove go flying past and pointed our pistol finger at it, as if to shoot.

Everyone except a woman named Kathy, who had never held a gun before, raised their hands.

"And you always get it, right?" Steve asked. "No one ever says, 'Ah, dang it, I was behind that one.' Trust me," he said, waggling his finger at us, "your hand's going to try to make you happy."

He said that the wiring is already in us to intercept that bird, and the only way to miss is if you do something to short-circuit that wiring. He was not giving us a New Age pep talk but explaining the marvels of physiology and neurobiology. The mind is like a computer, and as you're watching the bird's flight, if you allow your body to "watch" the bird, and don't do anything to disrupt that "watching" — stopping to squint at a bead at the end of your barrel, for instance, or cocking your head at some loose and goofy angle against the gun butt — well, then, your body will try to connect — *will connect* to where your eyes are searching. You don't have to go to school to learn this: it's already within us, after a hundred thousand years of reaching, and grasping, connecting body to sight. As Steve explained this, I found myself remembering two quotes. In *A Rough-Shooting Dog*, Charles Fergus quotes white advice on the act of shooting: "Grasp the bird, venomously."

And Thomas McIntyre, discussing the ideas of the Spanish philosopher José Ortega y Gasset: "According to Gasset, animals thought of as game are not hunted by chance, but because in the instinctive depths of their natures, they have already foreseen the hunter (before he even enters the woods), and have, therefore, been shaped to be alert, suspicious, and evasive." (Their shape, in turn, is what has molded our own — the wiring of our brains having been prepared for this pursuit.) And again according to the philosopher, the only adequate response to a being that lives obsessed with avoiding capture is to try to catch it."

*   *   *

"All day long, I'm going to be telling you to shoot at that bird's head," Steve said. "I won't be telling you to lead. Just try and shoot the bird in the head," he said, "not the tail."

This reminded me of something Tom said that has always bothered me. We were out duck hunting, and per usual, I was missing. Tom couldn't figure it out. "Shoot when their wings are *up*," he said, lifting both arms over his head to demonstrate duck flight, "not when their wings are down." I stared at him, understanding clearly for the first time how different we were: how there was this thing inside him that was not inside me. Shoot when their wings are up, and their breasts exposed? It's all just a bunch of splashing water and furious flapping, to me. Before that, I had kind of thought all people were pretty much the same.

Along these same lines, Steve spoke of being able to see the shot string itself — not the packing wad that is ejected behind the shot, but the string of tiny pellets themselves, swirling and shifting like a swarm of bees as they hurl at a thousand feet per second toward the quarry. "After each of your misses, ask yourself whether you were high or low, or behind, or some combination of the two. No one ever shoots ahead of a bird," he said.

It took me about half a day — the full morning — to believe him. "You can see the bird's *eye*," he said. "Try and shoot at the eye."

He told us how he shudders whenever anyone invites him over for a wild game dinner. All those shot pellets in the pheasant's rear end.

Most people see that big old tail on a rooster, he

said — it catches their eye — and they can't help but shoot at that. Their body can't say no to their eyes, so they shoot where they're looking: at the tail. Sometimes they get lucky and just barely clip the pheasant in the butt.

"Always try to miss in front." He showed us his trigger finger, then pointed to his head. When it's time to pull the trigger, the finger will take care of it.

It is all about *not* messing up. "Make this gun do what the bird's doing in flight," he said, "and get a good mount" (against your cheek), "and the bird will die every time," he said. "And shoot at the head." If you do those three things — cheek-to-gun mount, look down the rib, and shoot at the head — you won't miss.

"Point at the nose," he said. "Drill him hard." His words were quiet, almost hypnotizing, in the falling rain. Breath clouds rose from all of us, as if from animals in a stockyard.

He told us the three things again — mount snug, look down the rib, shoot at the head — as he would tell us a hundred, or maybe a thousand times. It's why the exercises in the mirror are so important. Just those three things.

"If you add one thing, or leave one thing out, you'll miss."

And then he told us the most horrible truth of all. "You have got to get to the point where you don't care if you hit the bird or not, but that you do the movement right."

Not care if I get the bird? Not care if I deliver it to earth for my beloved dog?

"If you do the movement right" — anchor to cheek,

look down the rib, shoot at the head — "the bird will die."

We hit a few more pigeons on the next round. He stayed as calm and steady as ever, but I seemed to detect a spark beginning to glow in him — a warmth, a pleasure, made noticeable not by its pronouncement but rather by its restraint, and the absence of comment, when we struck a pigeon. Sometimes the slightest of smiles.

Kathy, the woman who'd never held a gun, struck one, fractured it spinning in four different directions, and laughed out loud.

Steve fed us the shells slowly, one at a time, reaching into his deep pockets: the yellows for the twenty gauges, the reds for the twelves. The Candy Man. Slowly, and then quickly, we became addicted. It was like falling into a dream, where there was only the gun, and the shooting, and the clay pigeons flying against the rainy sky: a waking dream, through repetition.

Finally we were ready to learn.

I wondered how many times he has seen it before.

As if frightened of this letting-go — the speed of it, and the foggy *vaporousness* of it — I tried instead to pull out of that zone and regain consciousness. Even as the memory of success was being developed, I struggled against it. It was so startling to see some of the pigeons breaking when I shot that I wanted to be more conscious, not accepting that the two words, *conscious* and *aware,* are perhaps for some things incompatible.

I purposefully took a step back from that wonderful

feeling of submergence — a feeling like backing out of the deep end — and looked out at the gold and green forests of autumn, the snowy visage of the fog high in the mountains. It was almost as if I was *scared* of learning — or of not being in control of the learning. Scared of following it, rather than pulling it behind me like stones on a steel sled.

"It should be smooth and easy," Steve said, as if reading my thoughts. "I used to do it hard. Now I do it easy. If you ain't gettin' paid for it, don't turn it into a job."

He meant I was rushing the gun to my cheek too fast, then stopping to think.

After every miss, he arched his eyebrow at the misser — a gesture that, we learned, meant *Why'd you miss?* And we had to be able to stop and answer. *Poor mount. Behind. High. Low. Behind. Poor mount, behind, poor mount. Wasn't looking down the rib of the barrel. Behind.*

"I'm not trying to be mean," he said. "You'll be out in the field and miss, and you'll need to ask yourself why — and you'll need to be able to answer."

If you have trouble dropping into that dreamland of vaporizing pigeon-dust, Steve can also give you the straight scoop — practical directions on how to get there. If you insist, as I kept doing, on thinking about it, instead of just pasting them.

Steve asked politely for a gun: demonstrated the smooth lift. It's like he said: he wasn't teaching us to hit the pigeons, he was teaching us the memory of the movement.

"Pretend you're putting butter on bread — *spread* the barrel toward the bird."

"Pretend you're on TV and they're filming you, and they can just see you shooting — they can't see the bird. Swing real slow and easy like you're on TV."

"Pretend you've got a shot glass of Glenlivet on the end of that barrel, as you swing it. You know what happens if you spill Glenlivet?"

No, what?

"You go directly to hell."

Slowly, steadily, the clay pigeons died. It seemed that Steve allowed himself just the tiniest bit of pleasure, as we began to improve, but again, perhaps not: there was still so much work to be done, so much to be taught, so much to be learned.

"*Try* and shoot out in front of the bird. Try and shoot too far in front of the bird, on purpose. You cannot do it. It is an impossibility. Your body will not let you do it."

I struggled to prove him wrong. But the pigeons shattered, or vaporized. It was like a magic trick: as if he was demolishing them with some hidden remote control.

Sometime after lunch, the surprise of hitting one was replaced by the surprise of missing. We liked it. Slowly we were becoming addicted: craving our next turn in line; craving the next shell. Craving the next call, *Pull*. It became fun. Our muscles were learning, our memory. It was too easy.

*　　*　　*

By the middle of the second day, through the bonding of the shoot, if not the hunt, we were all good enough friends to be talking politics. Some of my urban classmates were confused by the fact that I am a hunter and an environmentalist both, and I felt like wailing, so vast seems the distance between us, and so short the time remaining in which to cross it.

One of Steve's teaching tools — his one and only prop, actually — was a little replica of the black and orange clay pigeon we'd been shooting at all day. The replica was about the size of a fifty-cent piece, which is about what the real pigeon looks like, over the end of your barrel, forty yards out — and sometimes before a shot Steve would align his toy pigeon at the end of our barrel, to help us visualize how to make this shot. If it was a crossing-left shot, he would place the toy pigeon just to the left of the end of the barrel — reminding us visually, in that manner, to shoot at the head. It was a little like a crutch, priming us beforehand with so specific a search image; but man, did it work.

Most of the time.

Occasionally, each of us would fall into a slump, and when one or the other did, it was for the rest of us a feeling like watching someone step through thin ice and disappear, or slide down a steep slope toward some awful abyss. There was the urge to reach out a helping hand — to pull your companion back into the land of the dream zone, and good shooting, sure shooting — but there was nothing that could be done, it was all internal, and we could only watch the shooter try to punch his or her way out of that little misery. It was horrible to watch — a previously smooth stroke, slow and confident, relapsing into a herky-jerky stabbing, complete sometimes with the wavering figure-eight at the end of the barrel — the barrel end drawing invisible ellipses *around* the bird, but not covering it — before and after each hit. After earlier achievements of grace, the reappearance of awkwardness embarrassed us, like the rudeness of some stranger. *Who invited you, anyway?*

What makes a good teacher, a great teacher? It was interesting to me, when one of my classmates hit a slump, to sit back and watch Steve watch the slumper. I don't know how many rounds we'd fired by this time — surely it was in the high hundreds — and Steve no longer asked us for an analysis after each miss, but instead just watched us try to sort it out on our own, as we would have to do in the future.

Kathy hit no slump. Steve noticed it, and commented on it — the point at which she crossed over into Dreamland. All the times before, she'd been letting Steve eject her spent shells, and reload new ones. At some point, after perhaps a dozen pigeons dusted, she began ejecting her own shells with authority and confidence, and held out her hand, asking the Candy Man for more. If it had been a competition, she would be outshooting us all. But it wasn't. It was just a process, a movement, a dreaminess and a steadiness. Sometimes to me it felt strangely as if the pigeons were swimming through the air, so slowly did they seem to be moving, and swinging the gun on them also felt like swimming — so easy. Kathy described it that way too;

she said that for her, it seemed as if the pigeons were "floating."

Steve just smiled. The pounding of our guns seemed to be lulling him, centering him.

When my own turn for a slump came, I fought it, of course. I tried to shoot my way out of it, but couldn't, and then I tried to think my way out of it, which certainly didn't work. In frustration, I asked Steve a bonehead question: Is there such thing as a "natural" shooter?

He simply laughed. He'd heard the question a million times. "For fifty thousand dollars," he said, "you too can be a natural shooter."

Finally, long after I'd given up — once I'd gotten to the point of not caring, and then some — I pulled back out of the slump. Steve let me shoot some more — enough to get my confidence back, and enough for my muscles to regain the memory of success — and then it was the next shooter's turn, and it was as if the slump never happened: as if it were only one page in a long-ago chapter.

The big question, then: it was the third day, and we were shooting doubles. How would this translate to the field? Would it translate at all?

Steve smiled. "Man, birds are going to be so easy, after this. You're not going to believe how easy they'll seem compared to the clay pigeons."

My heart leapt, dared to hope.

*   *   *

110

A storm swept across the mountains, rushing across the meadow toward us and bending the tall grasses like waves at sea.

Steve's back was turned to the storm. We were all gathered under an awning that the lodge had constructed for us, so that we could keep on shooting; even in the rain — so rare, for this time of year.

The wind caught the awning; lifted it, and the poles and struts that framed it, toppling the whole works. I cried out a warning to Steve just as the poles broke loose, but there was no time; the whole works came over on top of us, and one of the crossbeams struck him in the head.

He ignored the damage, joked that it was a good thing it only hit him in the head — but for a second, as the tarp wrapped around us and the wind howled and the crossbars flew, I saw a look cross his face — a tenseness — that made me wonder if the storm, for at least a few seconds, and the surprise of it, might have brought back at least some tiny glimmer of the war a quarter of a century ago.

After it was all over, we shared a drink in front of the fireplace at the lodge. Steve asked me to keep in touch — to be sure and let him know how my hunting season fared. I was scheduled to head to Washington in three days for a hunt.

And here is how it went.

On the first two days, I shot as well as I ever have in my life. The California quail looked like little whirring buzz-bombs, their wings spinning but bodies filled seemingly with helium. I seemed able to see every feather as they flew. I could see their eyes. I shot out in front of them; some fell. The chukhars fell too, including a double, which made me feel like alerting the media. A Hun tumbled at long range.

The third day, I reverted to my old tricks. I missed a lot. I missed a lot of easy shots.

The fourth and last day, I shot worse than I have ever shot in my life — which, as I hope you'll understand, covers quite a bit of territory.

And that is how the rest of the season went for me: erratic, but with some good days, whereas in the past, there had been none, as far as birds killed went.

Reviewing my season — my hits, my misses — Steve Schultz would say I need more practice, and more lessons, I suspect. And he would be right.

I told myself what I have been telling myself for years — what all men and women who miss have told themselves, in the thin consolation of an absence of birds: *Well, anyway, my dog still loves me.*

Fourteen

As COLTER and I crossed the mountains, the northern lights burned on the horizon as if some magnificent new culture were being born just over the next hill. The road hummed under my big snow tires. Colter slept with his head in my lap. The pups — Point and Superman, five months old, napped in their kennel in the back of the truck.

It was after midnight when we reached the motel. Room Two was open, as the new owners had told me it would be: I could fill out the paperwork in the morning. I ran the dogs (cold wind, bright stars — flagpole chain whipping the metal pole, clanging), then carried bags into the room, trying not to awaken the neighbors, who would be up before dawn full of adrenaline: an adrenaline I couldn't imagine at the moment. I just wanted to sleep.

Ten years ago I could not have imagined sleeping in when there was hunting to be done. But in the morning when I heard trucks rumbling in the darkness, and quiet voices speaking too-tense commands to dogs, I pulled the pillow over my head and slept deeply for another two hours.

I ate breakfast at the Bobcat Café, with the orange sunrise revealing purple and red mussel-shells of clouds. The other hunters were already out in the fields. Because I was wearing old denim overalls, rather than my fancy two-tone canvas bird-hunting pants, which my mother-in-law gave me last Christmas, the farmers did not take me for a bird hunter and felt free to say not particularly nice things about hunters and what they perceived, quite understandably, as an invasion.

I couldn't imagine knocking on someone's door before nine, at the very earliest. Ten seems more proper, but perhaps on opening day, the farmers would be expecting us . . .

I went back to the room and loaded the dogs. Colter seemed keenly interested in the country around us — remembering, I'm sure — but more mature, workmanlike, than last year. The pups, still sleepy, didn't have a clue. They were still more interested in wrestling each other than in separating and drifting off toward the wonderfully rank and infinite colored scent cones drifting in from over the horizon.

I stopped and gassed up at the Conoco and grabbed a cup of coffee. For the next hour or so I drove around on the back roads, watching huge flocks of roosters feed regally amidst the new-turned stubble, the black soil barely oxidized by even a day's worth of sunlight, as if the farmers had furrowed it to try and lay out a last feast for the pheasants just before our coming. Even the brown hens were beautiful, brown and gold and cream and white in the morning light.

I pulled over and filmed them with the video camera, then drove on.

I stopped at one of our old coverts and got permission to hunt. A lot of the land we used to hunt was posted orange now — leased for the first time ever — but this particular land was still open to the public. I thanked the owner, drove down toward a corner of his vast property, and stepped into the field.

It was windy as hell — steady winds of 30 miles per hour, gusts of 40. Colter began finding the birds soon enough, but they were wild as hares, running of course, but then scooching away whenever he pinned them. Colter was a little revved, barking and chasing them when they flushed, so that I could not shoot: but finally we got it all together and I was able to take a poke at a young rooster. It fell immediately, and Colter rushed over to it (against command) and began mouthing it, doing his weird-ass half-retrieve. I met him halfway — against the books — and I admired the first bird of the season, as all pheasant hunters admire each and every pheasant. The world around me is being eaten with a chain saw, but the coloration, the iridescence and hues and brilliance of pheasants will not change in my life, and will be like an anchor to hold on to; I cannot imagine an autumn, or a winter, in which I do not hold at least one sun-bright ring-necked pheasant.

I sat there with it a long time. Looking down in the field below I saw a group of hunters, a small infantry, heading my way. They were not wearing hunter's orange and were moving directly toward me, coming in at an angle as if to cut off my escape into the country ahead. Flocks of sharp-tails were getting up in front of them, barking their singular clucks of alarm, and pheasants too, roosters escaping in distant flushes, setting their wings and gliding in foolish curls directly across where Colter and I were crouched. They passed in flocks so low we could see the sun glinting in their eyes, could hear the wind cutting their wings. I held Colter by the collar and let them pass — you can shoot only three pheasants a day, and though I've never gotten my limit of any kind of bird, not even three grouse in an eight-hour day, I do not shoot: I was there to work Colter and, if there was time, the pups, and did not want to piss away the day with three birds gotten in three shots, while the morning was still young.

I placed the pheasant carefully in the back of my game bag and, breaking off crosswind to escape the posse, we hunted our way back out of the covert. Colter ran distant because the pheasants ran distant, rejoining me only a couple of hundred yards from the truck. A fancy truck stopped next to ours and an older man and a younger man got out with their guns. They waved to me and began walking across the field toward us. Colter, lost in the dreamland of scent, didn't see them, and I steadfastly ignored them. I was pissed that if Colter did find a bird, I couldn't shoot it,

due to this advancing backdrop of human protoplasm.
I was also frightened that if he found one, they would
take a swing on it, endangering Colter or myself.

"What kind of nose does your dog have?" the old
man asked.

"He's a fucking genius," I told him.

It turned out the old marauder had wounded a road
bird at daylight — he pointed to his husks, shining
bright and red in the road — "This is where I shot
him" — and so I turned Colter back into the field and
we hunted for the missing bird for perhaps twenty
minutes, the two strangers following me with their
guns aprop. They showed me where the bird went
down — no feathers — and by the way they were eye-
ing my rooster, it's clear they believed I'd already
picked up their bird.

I finally bailed out of there and headed for my friend
Mar's house. He lives at the end of a long drive shaded
by yellow-leafed cottonwoods, and he grazes cattle —
Black Angus — and doesn't have a lot of cover, but
sometimes the cattails along his irrigation ditches have
been known to give up birds.

He was up on top of some three-story earth-turning
machine when I drove up, and he was smiling as always. He took his time climbing down to visit. His
old father was up on top of another machine, working with wrenches. They were hatless in the wind,
dressed in oil-stained coveralls, *working*, smiling. Yellow cottonwood leaves blew past us in the wind.

Mar observed with pleasure that I had a new
truck — that I'd traded down for a rusting-out mud-

splattered '84 Toyota — and though he was still smiling, always smiling — "Hillbilly!" he called, greeting
me — he was in a fine and agitated state about all the
"doctors and lawyers" that were leasing up all the
land around him, driving over there in their fancy new
trucks wearing fancy new clothes and hunting with expensive dogs.

"It's not like it used to be," he said. He observed
with pleasure my old overalls, commented on them,
and I was glad I wasn't wearing those good pants, not
the first day out, though I also felt a little trapped —
what if I *wanted* to wear them?

Mar enjoyed telling his father that I'm an environmentalist — at first his father thought he meant I was
an *anti*-environmentalist, and launched into the stock-
in-trade harangue against regulations and urban elit-
ists and such — but Mar interrupted to tell him that
no, no, he's one *of* them. Mar's father stopped mid-
sentence, shrugged, looking surprised, as if a grizzly
or something more exotic — an oryx, or a tapir —
had wandered into their yard. He studied his son
with a look that said very clearly, *Well I always knew
you were a strange one, Mar, but befriending an environmentalist?*

"He's a tree-hugger," Mar exclaimed proudly, studying me as if I'm some fish he's caught — the novelty of
having such a person on their driveway, much less as a
friend.

"I used to be," I told them. "But now there aren't
any trees left big enough to hug."

Mar laughed and nodded. "You're right," he said.

"I took a drive through your country once. They didn't leave much, did they?"

"No," I said.

Mar said that he's always a little unsettled by hunting season. He's used to looking to the horizon — his ranch faces east — day after day, and never seeing a soul. Then pheasant season comes, and the fields are crawling with humans and their dogs. He pointed out to the road, where two shining new trucks were zipping up and down the lane, raising white dust.

"The sheriffs," he said scornfully. "This club leased a bunch of land and they have two of their members drive up and down the roads guarding it, making sure no one else gets on." Mar snorted. "They spend all their time driving. They've got land leased from here to the end of the world." He gestured to the horizon. "Soon as they get over there, it's time to turn around and come check it out over here." He shook his head. "A damn police state. Any of 'em come by here, I tell 'em they can't hunt. My land's only open to free hunters, not those dang doctors and lawyers. Course none of 'em ask anyway. They see that it's not posted and go right out onto it."

We stood there in the cold wind, the yellow rivers of leaves racing past, and talked for another fifteen minutes, about cattle, deer, wheat, corn, barley, alfalfa, timber, oil, gas . . . Mar's father kept working away, up there on top of that machine, and Mar kept glancing back at his own earth-turning machine.

Finally our conversation thinned — the wind was still blowing, as it would all weekend — and Mar pointed me down toward a field of his that no one has hunted yet. It was a green wet patch in the center of an otherwise sere landscape, about two miles distant.

Colter picked up the scent, despite the wind; worked to the bird, leaned into the scent cone — the bird flushed, a very big bird, I swung and shot without aiming — and the smaller feathers sprayed everywhere, it landed heavily and unmoving in a short-clipped field of winter wheat about twenty yards away. The odd juxtaposition of color — the brilliant pheasant and the emerald of the field — looked like what I imagine England or Ireland or Scotland to look like, not eastern Montana. When I picked the bird up, more feathers whisked away, blown steadily eastward by that ferocious wind pouring across the plains.

I stopped to see some more old friends. They were furious that some of their neighbors are leasing the CRP lands — getting subsidized by the taxpayers to let the land lie fallow, and then getting paid to lease that fallow land to private groups of hunters.

Land that might be worth only four or five hundred dollars per acre deeded can bring in forty dollars a year every year for ten years, for being held fallow under the CRP program. And there are farmers, landowners, who have amassed large holdings in this manner — a kind of time-delayed, slow-motion, modern-day land rush; a homestead act of lawyers and reverse manifest-destiny.

My friends had gone hunting earlier in the morning. Their black Lab was in the hallway, anxious to go back out; two pheasants were already hanging by their ankles, wings spread, in the hallway. Muddy boots were drying by a small wood stove, and a bowl of fruit was on the table. Bright leaves blew past the farmhouse windows: an illusion, as if all of eastern Montana were being covered with yellow leaves, though it is only around the farmhouses and along the creeks where such trees grow in any quantity, enough quantity to turn the sky to swirling yellow for a few days each year . . .

They welcomed me to hunt, though someone was already hunting their fencerow and cottonwoods, so I drove on toward another piece of land I have often admired where I have seen swarms of other hunters — and pheasants — but have never been able to catch up with the owner.

This time he was in, and said that sure, I could hunt it. He owns the square mile behind him, through which wanders a scraggly, brushy draw of wild rose and hawthorn, perfect for the rough old roosters to hide in after cruising his barley fields. Pockets like this — geomorphic scoops and shallows — that cannot be tamed, are few and far between in a landscape of such unremitting uniformity, but they hold the wildness that hunters seek.

The man doesn't farm the land anymore; his son does. He took me out and showed me his work shed. It's a lonely little building, about the size of a garage, and inside it was stuffed with carefully crafted wooden toys of every imaginable size and shape and sort. There were also table saws, band saws, jigsaws and other unidentifiable rust-colored pieces of machinery positioned about the room, but they were dwarfed by the stacks of toys surrounding them, rising to the ceiling. The machinery was all old-looking — polished and maintained, still functioning, but old-looking, with curves and shapes and scrollings not seen anymore, and the place looked the way I imagine Santa Claus's workshop would look.

The scent of wood and sawdust was dense in the dark, cool workshop.

Toy Man, as I think of him, wandered the narrow aisles of his shop, pulling down small dollhouses, little carved sculptures of tulips, alligators, coyotes, birdhouses, ducks, little wooden boxes that make quarters disappear — and tossed them to me so unceasingly that I barely had time to admire each one before it was time to look up and catch another that was being thrown in my direction. He told me I could take these things home with me, and I told him that my daughters would be thrilled.

He would not stop giving me things, and by the time I left, I was carrying two large sacks, one in each arm; *I* felt like Santa Claus. I told him I'd send books — he said he likes to read — but it was hard to imagine him having the time to do anything other than work with wood.

I stacked the toys in the truck and we stood out in the bright sun and cold wind and talked a while longer. He said he gets the wood from a factory about thirty or forty miles east of here. The factory builds the aluminum shells for satellites or something, and the wood comes from the shipping crates in which those parts are shipped.

122

Some of the wood is red fir from Washington and Oregon. The way he said *Oregon* made it sound as if it's light years away — *Brazil, Argentina* — and then I remembered that I was on the other side of the Divide.

I was very grateful for his generosity, but was also anxious to get back into the field. Still, he talked on, and so I shoved bird hunting further from my mind and relaxed and listened, even as the dogs in their kennels in the back of the truck stretched and whined, rattling their collars and rocking their boxes from side to side like caged thunder, mad drummers.

He told me that he never goes to craft fairs and such — that he likes to give his toys away. From the looks of his shop, it appeared he has a lot of catching up to do in this regard. I wondered if his toys were in every home in this county. I wondered what the density of the human population was here. Probably one, or less than one, per square mile. Maybe we were even statistically invisible.

He collected all sorts of things: rocks, stones, antlers, animal tails. I wondered if his propensity to collect was a response to the landscape — so severe and flat.

As Toy Man collected things, so too did his unfarmed gully collect pheasants. They leapt up before us, roosters all of them, in what seemed like unending succession, peeling away downwind — it was gusting to fifty miles an hour, all but impossible to hunt — like synapses of electricity, like momentary fragments or *thoughts* of pheasants, then nothing, as if the whole world had sped up, and we were whirling so fast that we could barely hold on.

I had no business hunting Colter in those conditions —

the dry wind was breaking apart and casting away the scent cones like an atom-smasher, so that he was having to ground-trail the running birds — but we hunted on anyway, into the gale forces, too stubborn to relax or pause.

That night, back in the hotel room, Colter, bone-weary from pounding the field and working into that wind, fell asleep immediately, snoring lightly, but the pups were frisky. Point, the beautiful ticked one, stood on the bed and stared at himself in the mirror, while Superman, glossy brown like Colter, lay on the bed and watched with unblinking fascination the soundless football game on the television. It got me to thinking about my life. I do not think it is diminished in any way, by virtue of my living so far back in the woods — it seems quite normal — but really, how normal can it be when your dogs have seen neither mirrors nor television before; when a trip to the Montana prairie becomes the equivalent of a visit to the big city?

A north wind awakened me, seeping in through the little cracks in the hotel room — slipping beneath the doorjamb, through the keyhole knob, and under the windowsill.

That morning I took a bird from Mar's cover. Even after my lessons, I am still such a poor shot that it always amazes me whenever I hit one. I don't think I'd have it any other way.

I got another bird later in the day from a vast CRP field — several thousand acres — on the other side of town. It's my favorite place in the world to hunt pheasants because it's on a ridge along a gorge — the river in that gorge looking as large and improbable as the Mississippi itself in that otherwise planar furrowed dirt — and as I hunt I can stare straight out across at the Rocky Mountains.

Colter pushed up a burrowing owl — the scent of owls fascinates him, and I love to watch their elegant, Halloween-spooky-lazy flight — and, a short distance later, feeding on the same grasshoppers, a small laughing flock of sharp-tails. I was distracted, staring at those mountains, and was unable to shoot, even when he stopped to flush and pointed a straggler. Sorry, boy. I should know better. Out in these fields, about every third time I find a burrowing owl, there are sharp-tails associated with it.

The afternoon slipped on. The sun was setting behind the Rocky Mountains, lurid red and pink and purple, and the stony walls of the mountains were violet and gray. I cannot understand why the natural world is so beautiful. I cannot understand why we do not fight tooth and claw to hold on to every last corner and vestige of its raw wildness, those last untouched places we still have in our possession. I regret having been so moderate in my defense of wilderness the first forty years of my life, but fortunately there is still a little time left to make up for it — though unfortunately, there is no longer as much wilderness to defend.

Colter was working a bird hard, zigging and zagging while I was still staring at the wall of the Rockies — the back side, the other side, of where I'd come from. The jagged peaks had already caught the year's first snow, the snowy peaks were shredding the wisps of orange and red clouds of sunset, and the mountains looked as if they were burning. Dusk was a moment away.

Colter accelerated, lunging up the hill, running a hot pheasant. The athleticism, the frenzy of his pursuit — the jags, slam points and turbo-sprints, each time the bird froze, then ran again — told me it was a rooster for sure. We were near the corner of the CRP, by an old string of wireless fence posts, where Tim and Tom and I took pictures of each other last year with our dogs and pheasants, with the mountains — again, like a wave — behind us. It had been midday, and as we'd been puttering with the cameras, Maddie had edged off and begun working a pheasant, a rooster, and had flushed it, and we'd all three just had to stand there with no guns in our hands and watch it fly away. It was one of the last pheasants I ever saw her flush, and we felt bad about it, certainly not for our sake but for hers — for letting down our guard while she kept pushing on, hunting . . .

It was in that precise spot, the same fencepost photo-corner, Colter was running a rooster, and I was hurrying along behind him, trotting toward that towering wall of mountains. I knew the pheasant was going to flush when he reached the end of the stubble, was going to launch himself up against that salmon sky and those holy mountains, and I for once was not going to miss — I was going to make that shot and watch that big rooster tumble into the open stubble, the black earth, and was going to go claim it. I knew with blood sureness that I would make the shot. As I ran toward that incredible sunset, following Colter's wild and acrobatic maneuvers, I felt the hair on my arms rising with a deepening chill.

It seemed impossible for Colter to be running Maddie's pheasant — but it seemed impossible, in the beauty of the day's last moment, for it *not* to be the same bird that we missed last year.

Colter pinned the bird: slammed on point at the bitter edge of the CRP. The dying sun was red in his eyes. He waited. I whoaed him and kicked at a clump of grass. Nothing. I kicked again. The bird was going to get up and I was going to shoot it. I felt extraordinarily calm with confidence. This moment would not be occurring in order for me to miss. I could barely make myself watch Colter's unblinking gaze at where his nose told him the pheasant was; I wanted to look at the mountains one more time.

I kicked at the grass again, trying to flush the pheasant. Colter's stub tail twitched once, twice — his signal that the bird had crept away. He broke point and thrashed wildly left and right along the line of stubble, trying to pick up the scent again, but the wind had carried it away, the rooster had snuck off — or perhaps it was not an earthly pheasant at all, but some ghost pheasant, something left over in spirit from last year — something hot and tremendous and furious, eternally alive and forceful, which, when pressured and pinpointed, simply vaporized.

It was dusk: no more hunting. My arms were still goose-bumped from the strangeness of the moment. My eyes stung with tears; my throat was tight. My dog and I headed back across the vast field toward our truck, as alive as we have ever been: our senses so sharp and whittled that we could barely stand it.

The mountains changed color beneath starlight. The beauty of it tried to take away my breath, and almost did.

One more day, my third day of not hearing any words spoken, other than by an occasional farmer telling me it was O.K. to hunt his land. I was just about to get used to it, but then it became time to go back home. It surprised me to realize how sociable I am — how much I missed human company.

Perhaps it's the country, over here on the east side, cracking me open like a shell, cracking open my dark woods persona. Landscape is like the forty-seventh chromosome, and over here it is as if I have a new identity. It was alarming, dangerous, invigorating, frightening. I would stay one more day, then head back to my other life.

The radio that morning said wind gusts of up to eighty. At first I had assumed it was a Canadian station and that they meant 80 kilometers per hour, which would have been about 55 miles per hour, but later I wasn't so sure they didn't mean miles per hour after all. Sometimes when Colter leaned directly into the wind, rather than casting back and forth into it, the gusts threatened to catch the thin keel of his chest and lift him up like a kite. He was always loping, never had more than one or two feet on the ground at any one time, so that the wind was giving him hell; airborne, he was powerless. The rough winds seemed to be carving even more flesh from his bones — only his noble head remained the same, so that compared to everything else, it seemed to be growing larger.

We found birds down in a marsh, among cattails, in ankle-deep water. They must have been floating on lily pads or something, or huddled on little mounds or hummocks, because when they leapt up into that wind, clawing and climbing twenty feet into the blue sky above us and then flaring downwind on that jet stream like supersonic spacecraft, they were dry: no water sprayed from their wings.

We found seven — all roosters, spaced precisely every thirty yards, like sparrows on a telephone wire — and I hit two: poor shooting as usual. Colter's face was latticed white with brush scars, his eyes, lips, nose shining red-raw from wind and brush, as was his belly; his scrotum was rubbed bright red too, so that back in the truck he couldn't find a comfortable position in which to even lie down on his cedar bed.

The opening day madness had passed, and I was glad. I *wanted* the fields to be empty of hunters — save for one or two or three friends. I could do without the mindless nimrods who cruise the gravel roads with street cannons bristling from the open windows, and yet I could imagine nothing more sterile or horrible for a country than to lose the few good hunters that it might have the good fortune to still possess, tucked back here and there, in this corner and that: in upstate New York, a suburb in St. Louis, the woods in Minnesota, a Mississippi swamp. It is a kind of cultural diversity, and yet many of my fellow liberals, fellow conservators, fellow environmentalists, would just as gladly see us vanish from the face of the earth.

It's a little frightening, to realize this, but also invigorating. It's good to be on the outside of things. It's where new things can be created and old things can begin again. A country needs good and fair hunters just as it needs wild roadless places. They can be a braid of its wild strength.

A pheasant flushed wild; I couldn't shoot, as Colter didn't point it. The wind was twisting us this way and that. We kept walking, leaning into it, hunting one last big CRP, trying against the odds to limit out: to get that third bird. It was late afternoon. I was working the edge, where the CRP borders some stubble, when a shiny new pickup truck came bouncing across the field, the driver heading resolutely, recklessly toward me. He was wearing camouflage, and stopped next to me with his window down.

"Do you know who owns this land?" he asked.

I knew the name, and had gotten permission from her in the past, but I was unable to reach her for this trip. The neighbors assured me that she was still allowing hunting on her land, which was still unposted.

But to answer this gentleman's question — no, I didn't know the lady, and no, I didn't have permission from her to hunt it that day.

"Well then, you'd better leave," he said.

I told him I'd do so immediately. I was mortified. I'm fanatical about not hunting unposted land without asking first. Montana law at that time said you could, but I thought it was a dumb and dangerous law. I apologized to the man, who was red-faced with adrenaline. I explained to him that I had tried to contact the lady. I wanted him to know — for his own peace of mind — that it was an honest mistake. Hunters have such a bad image, and it's clear that he's spent the better part of the day running people off this land. Explaining that he is a friend of the owner who is out of town for ten days, he apologized, too, and urged me to stay and hunt, and to get a pheasant.

We talked for a while about the hideousness of the road-hunting brigade, about how more and more land is being posted, or leased, which in turn places more and more pressure on those places that aren't posted.

I mentioned that I couldn't find anyone to make this hunt with me — that I usually come out here with my friends — and in a manner that will haunt me long afterward, the man laughed bitterly, said that he was in Vietnam and didn't have any friends either — that they're all dead.

He told me again to be sure to get a pheasant. He said they're out there. "You have a good hunt," he said. "You and your dog get one for me, buddy," he said.

And we did. It was a smallish rooster, but beautiful nonetheless. As I held it in my hand, I was a little surprised to discover that I didn't feel any different for having "limited" than I had all the hundreds of times before when I have not "limited." I was pleased that it didn't feel any different. I broke the gun open and we headed back across the field to our truck, over a mile distant.

In the day's last gold light, we stopped and watched an immense flock of Canada geese settling down into a stubble field for the night. Each one of them looked as large as a man, as they settled into a patch of copper light, grounded for the evening. A coyote walked through a slant of that copper light, walked to within a couple hundred yards of them, but he was no fool: the geese were larger than he was, and there were hundreds of them. I imagined he wanted only to admire their beauty: and he in turn, illuminated in that gold light, was beautiful.

Farther north, the patches of CRP thinned to nothing: there was only, as far as the eye could see, a quilt of black and gold: strips of fresh furrowed earth alternating with strips of wheat. Cyclones of dust swept like sheets of rain across the gentle flex of the land.

In the last few minutes of light, I took the pups for a spin along the slender ribbon of an irrigation ditch, where cattails, cottonwoods, and wild roses sprouted. This band of unplowed, unreachable wildness was less than forty feet wide, a thin seam of diversity at ecological ground zero.

A great blue heron leapt from the ditch and winged south with improbably elegant style; the pups stared after him with wonder. Ducks landed in the ditch ahead of us, whistling dusk silhouettes. Deer leapt out of the brush and bounded across the black field, disappearing into the darkness; a hen pheasant flushed in front of us, and the pups chased it a short distance before returning to my strident calls. All of these things hint what wildness this prairie landscape must have nurtured before it became one vast monoculture.

It was dark. The pups and I turned around and headed back to the truck, with the wind, now at our backs, propelling us.

We loaded up and headed home, not stopping until we got to Browning, where I bought gas and got a couple of corn dogs for Colter, who is addicted to them, preferring them with lots of mustard. It's a ritual every year; he gulped them down, and knew then that the hunt was over, and that he could sleep all the way home.

Fifteen

Bᴀᴄᴋ in the days when Colter had been going to Old South, Jarrett had said that some days Colter was like Michael Jordan, doing amazing feats that even Jarrett had never seen a dog do before, and then there were other days when he behaved more like Dennis Rodman: looping too wide, ranging too far, pretending not to hear the whistle, and even, on some nutty mornings, heading straight for the covey of birds and busting them as if out of sheer devilment. As if he just wanted to watch the excitement of the flush. Or to make sure Jarrett was paying attention.

Colter was one of the greatest bird dogs that ever lived. (You can doubt my word on that, but not Jarrett's.)

But to truly capture the essence of the dog, I have to include this idiosyncrasy. It happened only once in a blue moon, but for many traditional, tweedy sportsmen, once would be enough to dismiss a dog with a loud *harumph*. They'd prefer a dog that is more like a robot — a dog that would never, ever bump a bird, not by mistake (even if the dog had to become evermore cautious, gradually lowering its intensity level), and never, by God, on purpose, for the sheer adolescent joy of fucking up. They have spent the last hundred years line-breeding the perfect dog, or so they believe, intent upon all the things a judge can quantify in a trial, but overlooking, decade after decade, the intangible of heart. . .

Jarrett said that it really threw him, the first few times it happened — that at first he couldn't figure out why a dog of Colter's caliber would behave that way — but he figured it out, soon enough, and was tickled by it, amused rather than threatened. It was strange, he said, to see the two traits, greatness and mischief, so twined together, but he viewed it as a challenge, and was intrigued by it. The basic training process, the physical exercises, have become largely rote for Jarrett, and the real wisdom and value in his work comes from learning a dog's type and personality, and establishing a relationship: knowing when to push and when to back off. Knowing what can be demanded of the dog: the sky was nearly the limit. (The first time my friend Jerry saw Colter work, Jerry marveled at Colter's energy and said, "That dog's got a lot of *bottom*." Meaning, I think, you couldn't do anything that would make Colter want to *not* hunt.)

Sometimes, when we were hunting, after Colter made a staunch point, and I stepped forward to flush the bird, and fired and missed — missed twice, with both barrels, at close range — Colter would become frustrated and begin to yip, would even howl and scream. And after a couple of easy misses by me, he would sometimes throw an adolescent tantrum and take out howling across the countryside, chasing the bird to the horizon and then hunting on his own, galloping in huge wide-casting circles, bumping the birds rather than pointing them. It would be quite some time, often an hour or so, before Colter's nerves would calm down enough that he would return to my beckoning call and resume hunting, rather than howling.

Again, it is only because Colter was so great that I can tell you of this small weakness, which of course was not his weakness, but mine; one which he was forced, by the nature of the man-dog relationship, to accept.

Colter hunted well for Jarrett, it should go without saying, and he performed admirably when we were out in the field with Tim, who had, after all, spotted that first wild bird for him, that red ruffed grouse right at dusk, his rookie season. For some strange reason, however, he did not take to my father, who tends at times to be slightly critical, particularly with regard to subjects on which he has a high degree of knowledge and experience, of which hunting and bird dogs are two.

The first couple of times Colter went grouse hunting with my father up here in Montana, we found nothing; Colter ranged too far (easy to do, in these tight woods), galloped with his tongue hanging out, didn't come to the whistle, and didn't even find any birds to bump, much less point, which didn't surprise me: in a low year, I'll often hunt all day without seeing a bird. I really didn't think much about it. My father grumbled that I was being overly generous in my praise of the dog, but because we'd encountered no birds, there really wasn't anything to measure Colter against. There'd been no challenge. My father was dubious, but gave him the benefit of the doubt.

Down in Texas, Colter had been trained on quail, though they were slow-flying witless butterball pen-raised birds, not the lean wild quail that still inhabit the brush country and grasslands. To hunt wild quail in Texas, you need to own or lease some land. A lease costs around eight dollars an acre; and two to three thousand acres is about the minimum you'd need to hunt all season. Not many folks can afford to pay twenty thousand dollars a year for what Guy de La Valdene has called affectionately "a handful of feathers." But rich people need friends too, and my father was able to garner us an invitation to hunt with a friend of his who, despite being in the oil business, had still retained some degree of wealth. The friend owned over a hundred thousand acres — a small eco-system — adjacent to the legendary King Ranch in southeast Texas, and so one weekend in January I loaded Colter into his kennel and left the snows and subzero temperatures of Montana for the blue sky down near the Mexican border, near the Gulf. We stayed in the bunkhouse — my father, his friend B., and another of their friends, R., the three older men all over sixty, and me the youngster, not yet forty — and I have to confess that that first night around the camp-fire, before we'd been hunting yet, I bragged Colter up something fierce.

Being veteran oilmen, the other hunters had each seen and heard a lifetime of scams and shady deals and possessed acutely what Hemingway referred to as the "shockproof shit detector." Watching them listen to my tales of Colter's greatness, I could tell that their detectors were on alert. They were puzzled, though, by the apparent disingenuousness of my setup, for the proof of the pudding would be forthcoming very soon — the next morning! — and what kind of con artist would be mouthing off with such hyperbole when the day of reckoning was so close at hand?

They had never seen a completely liver-colored Ger-man shorthair before, and I thought this might work in Colter's favor, but R. said, "I don't like his looks," and B. added, "That's a pretty strange-looking knot on his head, kind of a knob-dealy."

"You'll see," I said. "You gentlemen are in for a treat. In fact, if you really knew what kind of a treat you were in for, you wouldn't be able to sleep tonight, you'd be so excited."

The oilmen sipped more whiskey, studied Colter some more, then looked back at the fire, noncommit-tal. I could tell that they *wanted* to dare to believe, but had become so encrusted by age and routine that they just weren't able, no matter how much they wanted to. Too dangerous. They held their tongues, though; they didn't disparage him. They played it safe. They gave him the benefit of the doubt.

138

It was exciting, being down there in a new landscape with him; like traveling to a foreign country. It didn't occur to me that what I would be asking him to do the next day would be the equivalent of delivering the Gettysburg Address in a language he had never spoken before.

I kept on bragging long after the fire had burned down to coals and the oilmen had begun to nod off. My sweet brown bomber dozing by the fire with his head in my lap. I couldn't wait. He would slay them. Even my father was starting to get excited about my sales job: he, who like the others was incapable of being bullshitted — least of all by me — was beginning to believe, against all his other instincts. Believing for that worst and most tenuous of reasons: because he *wanted* to.

The manner in which the older gentlemen hunted was to ride a jeep down winding trails cut through the brush, pulling a trailer of dogs behind them while one dog loped ahead, casting for scent.

When the dog encountered scent, and then crept in on the hidden, huddled quail and pointed them, the driver of the jeep would stop, and the hunters would clamber out, load their guns, and stride with alacrity toward where the frozen dog stood waiting. After one dog had run for a while, the driver of the jeep would stop, whistle the dog in, water the dog, examine its paws for thorns, and turn out another, fresher dog. It was a style of hunting to which I was unaccustomed, preferring instead the pace and intimacy of being down on the ground with my dog and my quarry. But you could run a lot of dogs and cover a lot of ground, and it was a good way to find a lot of birds, too.

When it was Colter's turn, he just *ran* — not casting ahead of us, but galloping along like a kid running cross-country, grinning and watching us sidelong with his tongue hanging out. It was his grin, I think, that was most aggravating to the older gentlemen, and B., our host and driver, seemed to be taking it personally, accelerating to try to keep up with Colter, who seemed in turn delighted by this strategy — a race — and so on down the bumpy dirt road we hurtled, not really hunting as much as just trying to stay up with the fabled, magical dog, even as everyone but me lost every inkling of faith in him.

Colter galloped through the thorny brush like a thoroughbred — not hunting a bit, just running. Running as if he didn't have a thought in his mind, and as if his blood no longer carried any instinct at all, only sheer contrariness. A demon hound, the other hunters saw now, a brown muscled genie brought down from Montana to unravel the very object of their longing.

Colter was busting birds as he galloped: veering course only slightly in order to run right over the top of them, exploding them into the heavens, at which point he would grin still wider, would throw his head back and bark at the sky, howling his success, and run even harder, so that now white flecks of foam were spittling from his jowls, and when I whistled and called and hollered for him to come in, to scold him and to water him, and to try to calm him down, he just grinned and ignored me, which I knew in the eyes of these veteran hunters was the worst thing a bird dog could do. Our morning's hunt deteriorated into a chase scene, with us following the bounding brown dog through the brush, with covey after covey of wild quail catapulting frantically into the sky.

We finally captured him with the aid of the herd of javelinas. When we caught up with him, they had him half-surrounded, tusky boars and angry sows and half-grown shoats, and were facing him, clicking their tusks, while he was crouched and growling with his hackles raised. I jumped out of the jeep and hurried into the brush with my shotgun, hoping to ward off the fight, and to my relief the javelinas turned and raced off into the brush.

I took hold of Colter by the collar and led him back to the trailer, hosed him down and watered him. He was as hot as a bed of coals, his breath a blowtorch, and as an excuse to the other hunters I offered up the notion that perhaps Colter was having trouble picking up the birds' scent, with the strange climate so new to him, so hot and dry.

We put him in his kennel and resumed hunting with the other dogs, none of whom appeared to have any trouble with how hot and dry it was, though I had to say that after watching Colter's exuberance and ath-leticism, watching the other dogs creep and prance so tentatively, so leery of making a mistake — so without style — was about as exciting as watching old men play croquet. I would rather have watched my dog run like the wind, any day, even if it meant passing up a few opportunities at birds. Being a guest, however, I kept my thoughts to myself, and eventually, we got in a little shooting.

As we hunted with the other dogs, I kept pondering on what had gotten into Colter: why he had turned so demonic. I kept bragging on him, too; I wouldn't just let it drop, and let these other hunters go away believing, so mistakenly, that he was a dud. In my mind, a hypothesis began to take shape, and later in the day, I cautiously proposed it.

"He's such a sweet boy," I said, "that I think he was freaking out, panicking that we were going to drive off and leave him. He's never hunted this way before. Maybe if I get out of the jeep and hunt on foot, while y'all drive behind us, he'll calm down."

Bless their old hearts, you could see them wanting to believe: knowing that they shouldn't, knowing that they'd already seen more than they needed to, but hooked, nonetheless, on the idea, or the *possibility,* of one of the world's greatest bird dogs appearing into their lives from out of some near-mythical land of glaciers and ice bears.

They gave Colter — gave us — one more chance.

Of course Colter didn't care if the Queen of Sheba was giving him one more chance; or rather, he *did* care, and was only too delighted to fuck things up again, running even wilder, grinning and mugging even more maniacally, and busting just as many quail as before — busting in his second brief foray more coveys than all the other dogs had found all day cumulatively, so that I understood at that point (and I think that the other hunters did, too) that there was nothing at all wrong with his nose. On the contrary, they realized that I was right, that he probably *could* smell every bird in the county, even which way the wind was blowing.

My father suggested that I put Colter up for the rest of the day, which I did, speaking sternly to him as I did so: "Colter! What has gotten into you? What do you *mean?*" It was a kind of language which, to the old-school hunters, was doubtless the equivalent of my counseling Colter to take a few deep breaths before trying to get in touch with his inner feelings; and I could tell by the way the three other hunters looked off fiercely in three different directions that they were thoroughly disgusted by both dog and man alike.

The younger generation, I could hear them thinking, *it's just not what it used to be, in the old days . . .*

A postscript, as if any were needed. That night, around the campfire, with all the "true" hunting dogs asleep in their kennels and Colter lying beside us, four men and one dog watching the fire, Colter got up and wandered off into the starry night. I would have thought he would be too whipped from his peregrinations to have any jauntiness left in him, and figured he had just eased off to take a pee, but I was mistaken; when he did not return after a few minutes, I called for him, but he did not return. I stood up and walked out into the darkness myself and called louder, but still he did not respond.

"Oh, God," my father said, "he's probably out running deer." The other hunters groaned, particularly the ranch owner, who had planned to take some other friends deer hunting later in the week.

"No," I said, "he won't run deer. He's scared of them. He's probably out hunting quail."

"Oh please," said R. "Spare me."

B., the ranch owner, said nothing, just got up and went off to bed. After a little while R. retired too, and it was just my father and me, waiting for Colter to come back — "Don't worry," my father said, "he'll be back" — and then, after my father went to bed, it was just me and the campfire.

I got a blanket and lay down there by the coals, and a little after midnight, Colter returned. I could tell he'd done something wrong, because he didn't come bounding straight back, but instead was kind of circumnavigating, staying just on the outer boundaries of firelight. There was a rustling in the brush, too, as if he was pulling something, and when I got up and went with my flashlight to go see what it was, I nearly retched.

He had found a dead calf and dragged the carcass back to camp. I could tell right away that he hadn't killed the calf himself, thank God — it had been dead for a few days — but such was his beastliness in the eyes of my hosts that I knew I might have trouble convincing them of that.

I went and found a shovel, and dragged the calf far back out into the brush, and buried it deep. I knew coyotes would probably dig it right back up, but by that time Colter and I would be long gone, never to return — never to be invited back — and I could only marvel at my luck that the other hunters had not still been sitting around the fire when the great chesty hound had come scuttling back in after a night out on the prairie, returning with game twice his size, his eyes shining red in the firelight.

Sixteen

ANOTHER YEAR PASSED, and Colter was blossoming like a rose. We spent the first week of bird season skulking around in the wet woods of the Northwest, prowling for grouse — ruffed, spruce, and blue — and Colter blew through everything, then leapt dancing on his hind legs howling and yowling after the grouse flushed. *A rose?* you might say, and I will say, *Well, in my mind anyway, he is beautiful.* I am convinced he will learn to point those spooky grouse yet. It just may take ten or twelve years.

Point and Superman were yearlings by this time. Point, the speckled little stylish one — sensitive, like a little poet, but built like a bull — was too valuable for me to mess up: I'd borrowed against the children's college fund to send him to go train with Jarrett.

Superman, however — brown as a fresh deer turd, the same color as his four-year-old brother, Colter — well, let's just say that I felt comfortable working with

Superman myself. There was nowhere to go but up. Superman, like Colter, was the gangly runt of the litter. Unlike Colter, however, who metamorphosed into this strapping muscular brown stud, Superman has remained scrawny, puny, and goofy as well. He reminds me of that disturbing little boy (modeled after Truman Capote) who played Dill in *To Kill a Mockingbird*.

He's sweet, though, with luminous green eyes and long eyelashes and velvety ears, and he has this incredible kind of Mr. Magoo luck. Though he can't find birds with his nose, he has an uncanny ability to blunder right across wherever they are hiding, often stepping on them, which terrifies both him and the birds. Already in the first week he had found a huge covey of blues in this fashion, as well as a good young covey of ruffeds. If you don't get too picky about these sort of things, he has the ability to put meat in the freezer. Some days I had half a notion to try to convert him into a flushing dog, though I could never let Jarrett know about it.

I had permission to hunt five hundred acres of CRP down in the Missouri River country. A friend had assured me it was fantastic, though he'd never hunted it himself. So, dreaming of perfection, a full limit of a mixed bag — doves, Huns, sharpies, maybe even a sage grouse — we headed east toward the ocean of grass seven hours away. Colter and Superman rode in the front with me, nestled together, until Superman developed a vile flatulence and was banished to the back — I could tell the reasoning was incomprehensible to him — while Colter, the old veteran, managed to maintain a tight sphincter, and was allowed to remain in the cab.

The distance, the gulf, between a good dog and a not-so-good dog is vast and immense.

We drove through the night in the bouncy old truck, watching the stars. There were no other cars after midnight, and I savored the loneliness of the black night. We drove with the windows down, to feel the brace of cold air as well as to try to eradicate Superman's lingering odor.

I don't mean to bust on him so much, but sometimes his goofiness, his un-birdy-ness, takes my breath away. In his defense, I must say that there was never a happier dog in all of the world.

Once over the Divide, we followed the train tracks east through one small town after another, silo after silo, driving into the September dawn. When we finally stopped for gas, we were in a new country, country we had never hunted before, and there were trucks full of hunters and dogs all around us, also gassing up. The place I had been told to hunt lay another two hours south, and I wondered if all those other hunters were headed there too.

We nodded and said hello to one another, none of us daring to divulge anything more (was it this way for hunters in caveman times?). My dogs have the habit of riding for long distances with their noses smushed up tight against the windshield, squinting out at the country ahead like figureheads on the bows of the old ships. Their damp noses slide this way and that at every little bump in the road; over the course of a long journey, they usually succeed in painting, with smeary, waxy dog-mucus, their entire half of the windshield an opaque scum color. When I took the gas station's squeegee and applied it first to the outside of my windshield but then, still dripping, to the doggy interior, I could tell that the other hunters were a bit taken aback, and when they asked where I was from, I told them the truth, "*Yaak.*" I could see by the way they edged away that they had heard of the place, and that they believed what they'd heard about it.

I finished gassing up, paid, and pulled out of the parking lot. Everyone else turned left — heading farther east — while we turned south. They all had Brittanys and Labradors and were grinning as if they knew something but weren't going to tell us.

You know that a man who will hunt with a dog like Superman — if it can be called hunting — doesn't really care if he shoots too many birds or not. And that's what I was thinking, when I crossed the big Missouri, and rolled deeper into new country. A hen pheasant scooted across the road ahead of us, but then changed her mind and came scooting back; a bad decision, a mistake.

Feathers swirled everywhere. I stopped, pulled over, and went back and picked the bird up and put it in the ice chest. When I asked Jim, the owner of the land where we were headed, if there were a lot of birds this year, he said there were so many that people were hitting them on the roads, and I had envisioned using them, if need be, to help fill my limit. I really like the taste of wild game.

I met Jim and Pat, his wife, in town. When eastern

Montanans meet western Montanans, we examine and visit with each other like distant cousins — friendly, but curious, certain that just as there must be inescapable similarities between us, so too must there be vast though perhaps hidden differences: all landscapes carving, as they do, with a unique blade, in a unique pattern.

Jim drove me out to the property. He and Pat were living in town for a couple of years, renting the farm out to a young family. It's Jim's grandfather's homestead — an island of the last century hidden out here against the end of this century. Even if the dogs and I didn't see one bird, it would be yet again an honor and privilege to hunt this old homestead. It's the kind of place I want my daughters to know about, and I was anxious to bring them out here sometime to see it.

The corrals were ancient weathered wood and iron, pitted by a century of ceaseless, merciless wind, but neatly kept, and within them were well-cared-for sheep and horses and a milk cow. I had let Colter and Superman out to stretch and when two of the woolly sheep wandered over to examine Superman and touched noses with him, he sniffed them, trembled for a moment, then bowled over backward, as if snatched by an invisible stage crook, and scampered back to the safety of the truck. It's strange how two dogs with the exact same parents can turn out so totally opposite.

Jim showed me the immaculate tack room — oiled saddles, bridles, and halters all in their place and at the ready — and I made the horrible mistake of referring to the little room as a "shed." There was a pause, but he was courteous enough to say nothing, forgiving my deep-woods ways.

There was one stock tank on the property, and in warm weather — the forecast was for a high in the upper eighties — that's where any birds would be. I thanked Jim and Pat and headed over that way. There were perhaps five hundred doves clustered around the tank, and the dogs and I stopped and listened to the flapping of their wings as they rose to depart. Colter was such a pro that he paid them no mind — his interest lay solely in the ground game — and neither did Superman, though in his case it may have been because he is constitutionally unable to take notice of any kind of bird.

There was a rusty old pump rising out of the field of CRP, and I worked the handle for a while, until finally a stream of rusty water gushed out. Even after the water cleared up it still had a yellowish tinge, and I looked out over the coulee at the big river below and realized that the water was coming straight from the Missouri. The dogs lapped it up as happily as if it were champagne, and, for some reason I couldn't explain, it pleased me that my dogs were drinking from the Missouri for the first time.

I put young Superman in his kennel with water in the shade beneath the dropped tailgate of the truck. Carrying a gallon of water in my daypack, I set out across the prairie with Colter, who immediately lit out at greyhound speed, grinning his big grin. The slashings of his casts as he rocketed back and forth in front of me seemed capable of setting the prairie on fire: he sent up a long roostertail of cut and clipped vegetation wherever he went, cutting a swath. Maybe it's wrong to look ahead to the days, years distant, when he'll slow down sufficiently to be a good woodland grouse dog. His glory is in the wide-open throttle, and in the moment. I knew I should get over to this big country more often.

A flock of doves exploded from cover and I swung and shot — Colter was already far away — and I was surprised, as always, when one of the birds fell. It was the first time I'd ever hunted doves in Montana, and as soon as I shot I could tell I hit the bird — it swerved, faltered, then flew hard a short distance before settling back to earth, falling upside down like a poorly thrown paper airplane. I do not mean to be disrespectful of my quarry, and later, when I was plucking the scant light feathers from its body (it's easy to see why the first frost pushes them south), the deep red chest meat, almost like that of a deer or an elk, bespoke a heroic endurance.

I called Colter back in and he helped me find the dove. He pointed it but wouldn't retrieve it, wouldn't even pick it up and mouth it, as he does with pheasants and grouse. As a puppy he used to retrieve, but as he has matured and gained more experience and had more birds killed over him, he's done it less and less. For a long time it bothered me, but I learned to focus on his talents, not his shortcomings — and I have come to see that he considers retrieving beneath his dignity. Colter is so muscled, now in his fourth year — such a stud — that it would humiliate him to spend time ferrying the birds back and forth to me. His job is to find them and pin them; my job is to shoot them. All the other tasks lie somewhere between those two extremes, and if the birds are to be gathered up, plucked, cleaned, cooked and eaten, then that responsibility is going to have to fall to me. He has committed himself to the discovery, pursuit, and pointing of the birds, and to diversify into other aspects of the hunt would reduce the white-hot fury, the headlong nature of what he does best. I picked a pointer, not a retriever. People don't bellyache because a retriever doesn't point, do they?

It was too hot to run the bomb-machine more than fifteen or twenty minutes. I stopped and watered him — he was lapping water from my cupped hand, panting, yet impatient to get back to the birds, and I poured water over his broad brown skull and trickled it all down his backbone. The water pooled for a moment between the twin points of his bony haunches, then parted and slid off on either side. He shook enthusiastically, all floppy-limbed in that awkward hound dog way, then set off again, ceaselessly hunting, but I headed him back to the truck, where Superman was snoozing.

Because Colter was drenched and I did not want him nastying up the passenger seat, I made the mistake of putting him in the kennel with Superman. As we drove off over the bouncy road, searching for a new place to hunt, I heard a snarling and tussling, a thumping — a yelp — and when I stopped I saw that Superman had a slash just beneath his eye, from which welled a crescent of blood, bright red in the sunlight. I soothed Superman, but didn't scold Colter; it was my fault, squeezing him in with the youngster like that.

We hunted again, into the sun, but still couldn't find any upland birds. I was able to shoot another dove, and began to consider how it would taste fried, with cream gravy.

Back at the truck, I emptied the melt-water from the ice chest over Colter's head and back. Then I took Superman out onto the prairie for a spin — more to exercise him and expose him to the vastness of space and sky and ground underfoot, than with the hope of finding any birds. Perhaps traveling this landscape will unlock some ancient, hidden message and he will blossom miraculously into even one-tenth the genius that his brother is.

We pressed on, into the heat, with blue sky all around us. Afterward, I hosed him off too, and, bleary-eyed from the all-night drive, we headed to the little town to look for a motel where we could check in and nap in the heat of the day.

On the banks of one of the wide rivers that flows into the Missouri, we found a tourist court kind of place, with twelve little cottages, stark white beneath the still-green murmurings of riverside cottonwoods, set in green lawn with sprinklers whizzing. Wild roses grew all around the cottages, and white picnic tables were set out on the lawn beneath the giant cottonwoods, and the whole place was vacant — we would be the only guests.

The lady at the counter said that the room would be twenty-five dollars, but that there was also an additional charge of five dollars per dog.

"Ahh," I said, reaching for my billfold, "you're killing me."

There was a fan in the room. The windows were open. Superman pranced back and forth, up and down from the floor to the bed and back, like a kid on a trampoline: executing fancy twists and flips over the back of the infinitely more mature Colter. I collapsed onto the creaky old bed, which was so soft and ancient, so spineless, as to be more like a hammock. Colter hopped up and lay down next to me, with his head stretched out on the pillow, and Superman wriggled in and draped himself across both of us — this was clearly his favorite part of the hunt.

Colter sat up and leaned over and licked the wound on his brother's face, tending to it with great concern, as if having no earthly idea of how it got there in the first place. He looked over at me then, and I studied him back, trying to see across that gulf between us — the one that does not let me understand the gulf within him: his placidness, now, versus his maniacal otherworldliness, when he's pushing a pheasant, run-and-gun, tearing up the brush, or working his way like a missile toward the ripe scent of sharp-tails.

I cannot fully grasp how he can have two such different lives — one he spends waiting, and then the second, higher, supercharged life into which he ignites every autumn.

He laid his head back down on the pillow with a groan and began to snore. He had made it through the boredom of summer and now he had a partner who was going to take him hunting as much as he absolutely could.

"This is the best time of year, boys," I said to them, just before I sank into unconsciousness.

Later in the afternoon, into the cool of the evening, we had only a couple of hours of light left in which to work, but they were good hours. Colter took me down into the cattails below the pond where he put up a gaggle of pheasants, one after the other, like a magician producing white rabbits from out of a hat. They were all hens, and it wasn't pheasant season anyway, but it would be soon, and I could barely stand the wait, anticipating it. One more month.

Still no sharp-tails, and no Huns, either. We took another dove. I didn't care if we found anything or not. It was just so damn great to be out in such open country with my dogs.

Closer to dusk, pheasants began flying into the CRP for the night — again, strangely, all hens — and when I saw a flock of six scoot across the road in front of us, I stopped and put Superman onto them. Colter wailed and shrieked his disapproval, but it was Junior's turn. I took Superman right across the path where the pheasants crossed — he lowered his nose to the ground with some interest, as if he planned to dig a hole there — but then he moved forward into the CRP, moving for the first time with a little authority and purpose, though whenever he got too far out from me — twenty yards — he grew nervous and came scooting back in.

Gradually, though, the cones of scent drew him farther and farther out, and with greater strength. In some places he began to false-point — a problem I'd never had with Colter, and which might show a lack of confidence — and sometimes, after false-pointing, Superman would grow nervous and run back and hide behind my legs, peering out first around one leg and then the other, before I was able to coax him back out into the great wide world, and forward.

We pressed on. I could see him gaining confidence as it first began to dawn on him — like coals being kindled by a steady breeze — that the bird was running away from him, that the bird was supposed to be frightened of him, rather than the other way around.

It became a game. He followed the scent in quick, gluttonous casts — swinging hard left, hard right, as if possessed by some fevered vision — and it was a beautiful thing to see, as I ran along behind him. And beyond my joy at the beauty of the sight, there was relief, too. For a year and a half, as I had listlessly trained him on pen-raised birds, and Superman had showed little or no response to them (aside from sometimes stepping on them), I had been wondering more and more if there was something terribly wrong with him: if maybe, tiny as he was, his brain was somehow stunted or undeveloped, as well as his ambition.

Superman was flying above the CRP though, in foxlike leaps and bounds, so that if there *were* a cape attached to his neck, he would have looked like his namesake. I hurried to keep up with him — with them, dog and pheasant — but it couldn't be done, and finally I just stopped and laughed and watched them accelerate as if into infinity, relieved that Superman was being born: that the bird, that one bird, was unlocking something in him.

I watched as in the distance he finally wearied and then pinned the bird with a tentative point. He held it, surely unconscious of what he was doing and completely oblivious of my distant, silent approval, doing it only for himself and the bird — it would take me many hunts to work myself into that equation — and from his imprisonment in the truck, Colter howled with indignation. He was not made to be a bench-warmer. I remembered that he, too, was the runt of the litter, but developed into a warrior. It seemed too far a piece of country for Superman to travel, but who knows? He too may get there yet.

The pheasant — a hen — flushed, and Superman held steady and watched it depart, though true to his nature, with an inquisitive, almost philosophical look, rather than the staunch mortal agony with which the Brown Bomber would have watched.

Dusk fell, and, feeling like the richest man in the world — possessing the finest bird dog in the world, and with new pups to train behind that great day, and plenty of years in which to hunt them, and plenty of country in which to hunt them — I called Superman in, and we headed back to the motel.

In the room, I fed and watered the dogs — Colter tried to show Superman the trick of drinking out of the toilet, but Superman was either too slow or too finicky to learn it. I went over to the little restaurant across the river, where I ordered a steak and eggs and pancakes. I could barely stay awake. I didn't read the paper, didn't read a book or anything; I just sat there, tired from the drive, and from the miles of walking, and getting older, but not minding it too much, not in bird season; and in terms of time available to me to hunt, and open country, and dog-power, I was flush. How could anyone dare quibble about a little advancing age? And it's better today than it's going to be tomorrow, or the next.

When I got back to the room, the dogs, brown twins, were overjoyed to see me. It was a quarter to nine. It felt good not to have spoken to humans almost all day. In five minutes I was asleep, with the dogs strewn all over me as if protecting me. I tried to remember if I ever had the fire about anything the way Colter does for birds, for hunting. There was a moment down in a coulee that day in the heat, even after I had watered and splashed him, he had been gasping so hard from racing up and down the near-vertical walls, that his lungs were pounding inside him like a bellows, and I knew that he would have gladly run himself to death, if I had given him half a chance, half a bit of encouragement to do so.

In two minutes I was asleep.

I dreamed no dreams.

I slept late in the morning. I had intended to be up at five and in the fields at first light, before the day began to warm, but it was almost seven o'clock before I was awakened by the sunlight through the curtains, and through the cottonwoods.

A piece of lemon meringue pie and a cup of coffee for breakfast, and we were out in the field, devouring the autumn. Less than a minute into our first morning run, Colter found a small flock of sharp-tails. He pointed them, one by one — my God, I'll never get tired of seeing that, never, and as they got up, and flew away clucking and laughing, I had what I thought was a good bead on each one, they looked so large and slow that morning. But I missed, as usual. Colter pretended not to care. The morning was young and still cool.

We headed over to a forty-acre spur of CRP off to the east, where Jim had said we might find sharp-tails. I walked briskly to keep up with Colter's bold casts. It was a beautiful, awe-provoking thing to see, the way he *consumed* that little forty: scouring it left to right — catching every molecule of cool scent — in less than ten minutes, maybe less than five. He was like some mythic beast that could eat the world. Two or three hundred acres of CRP would be just right for a warm-up. He ate this forty like a bonbon, and then we turned back into the larger CRP across the road, where, over a small rise, he pointed a rooster. I could see only the top of his bony head, holding staunch.

The rooster flushed, flew north. We turned south, back toward where the sharp-tails were, hoping to find a straggler. Colter stopped on the way and locked up on another bird — I stepped forward and flushed it: a hen pheasant. He held staunch, and I stepped closer, saw a second hen — still he held — and I came still

160

closer, and a third hen flushed, and finally he relaxed his tail, wiggled it to let me know that he'd counted them, and that's all there were.

While he had been on point, chocolate brown amidst the gold wheatgrass and the bright blue sky, a lone Canada goose had flown overhead, right behind him, looking down at him — not forty feet up and headed, I supposed, for the Missouri below. The goose looked huge in the sky, as large as Colter himself. I was tempted for a moment to direct Colter's attention to the goose, so beautiful was the sight — Colter had never seen a goose up close before — but I let the goose fly on, silent and unobserved, and we turned and headed off.

Later in the day, once the heat had begun to bake the world, I let Superman out for another practice run, and though he started out tentative again, he warmed once more to the strange lures of scent, and ended up pointing a young rooster. At first I thought it was a false point — the bird would not flush — but Superman would not release. It was the first time he'd been staunch in his life.

In training, on the rare occasion when he'd pointed, he was usually hunched over, with his back arched and his nose to the ground — as if he were preparing to take a dump. Other times he would lie down on his stomach to "point" — but it seemed possible, from this one tensed crouch, anyway, that a style might have been *trying* to develop.

I finally spied the rooster — too young to fly —

beneath the brush. I kicked at the brush, and it scooted. Superman trailed it to the horizon, where he finally lost it in that vast sea, and the heat.

He might make a dog yet. Already, stunted as he is, he was a better dog than I am a hunter. Which, thankfully, is not the point.

Goldfish swirled in the stock pond. Jim had said kids put them in there when he was in grade school, nearly forty years ago. I showed them to Colter, who seemed properly impressed, and we watched them for a while. A dove flew past, and I shot and missed. I never cease to marvel at how such a great dog as Colter ended up with such a dipshit of a hunter. I guess that whoever or whatever decides such things knew that I would love him.

Three more images, from that day:

A young girl, no more than nine or ten, riding a pretty rank horse around and around in a corral surrounded by sagebrush under that blazing sun, while her mother watched. The horse burdened with all sorts of heavy leather saddlery: the sun sapping and gentling the horse. Every time I passed by there, she was walking that horse around the corral under that blazing sun, taking a bit of the feist out of it. A beautiful horse, muscular as a titan, with that balding moon-face that can often mean too much spunk.

A water break, sitting on the tailgate parked out in the middle of nowhere, and kind of glazing out: staring at the ground, the dogs panting in the shade below me. I was watching a grasshopper and thinking how acutely aware I was of how extraordinarily content I was — how happy — and aware, conscious, of the great depth of the happiness. I was feeling the autumn and heat mixed together, watching that grasshopper, and thinking how short and irrelevant everything is: it doesn't matter who or what you are, or what you accomplish, time is going to level it all to dust almost immediately anyway.

It was a calming, reassuring realization, and I was a little embarrassed by the simplicity of the thought, banal as a greeting card. But I was happy, and beyond happy; at peace. It didn't matter if I ever did anything worth a damn. It didn't matter if I ever hit another bird. It was all dust, but God, I was happy.

Colter pointed, then bumped, the biggest flock of sharp-tails I'd ever seen. Easily forty, maybe fifty birds. I thought he had gone over to the pond to get water. I was sitting on the side of a coulee resting. The birds flew right down the coulee past me, and directly overhead, like some kind of miracle. I stood up and started firing — click, click, no shells — fumbled a load in — birds were still passing me in clouds, laughing and cackling — and I swung and fired, missed, took my time and picked out a new one, and fired just as it disappeared over the top of the coulee; my shot struck gray dirt, raised a puff of dust.

More birds were coming. I reloaded, fired at one overhead — missed — then swung on the last passerby and hit it. The bird rose straight up — all the others continued east — and it hung there, hovering, wanting to go on, but unable, before finally settling down along the fence.

I called Colter over to hunt dead. He did, and soon enough found the bird. I had reloaded, and when the bird flushed again, healthy and recovered — flying hard — I shot, missed, shot again, and finally it tumbled. I sent Colter over to fetch it, which of course consisted of his mouthing a few feathers off of it, a kind of laying-claim to it, and then he galloped off to hunt anew.

Our first sharp-tail of the year.

The third thing. Our last run of the afternoon, down in a coulee. We bumped a big buzzing flock of Huns, which must have reminded Colter of his training on bobwhites in Texas. I drew a good bead, picked the bird I wanted to hit, and fired, twice, missing it cleanly — behind it, I supposed, though the shot had felt good and true, and I'd thought I was going to drop one; I'd been confident, for once.

I think Colter felt the same way — that unspoken communication between us so sure and developed that he felt my confidence, and shared, for once, my disbelief, that I had missed.

After I had fired, as we both stared down the coulee in the direction the Huns had gone, an autumn-weary grasshopper sprang up from the sage, rising slowly into the air. Its wings filled with light as the afternoon sun struck it, and strangely, it made no sound. So slow was its illuminated ascent that it looked for all the world like a stray, loose feather rising on an updraft. Colter saw the light-filled grasshopper and took three careful steps toward it — it was still rising — sniffing the air to see if it truly was a feather, *wanting* to believe it was a feather; and wanting, as ever, to believe in me, despite my many faults.

Seventeen

Deep into winter, almost to the edge of spring — a long way from any hunting season — I'll occasionally dream of pheasants, brilliant roosters, exploding from the snowbound stubble of cattails — big pheasants, blue sky above, a red barn, rusting farm machinery in the background.

They always catch me by surprise, flushing after I have walked past them. In the dreams, Colter is off somewhere. I have become separated from him, and am on my own — and sometimes, despite being startled and unprepared, I make the shot. Usually, however, I miss. Those dream birds are the hardest ones to hit.

Eighteen

THE NEXT WEEK, back home, I cut my knee badly with the chain saw while thinning brush. The blade had torn through almost to the kneecap, slicing open the bursa over the patella, so that it would not stop bleeding. I finally had to go in that night for stitches. The next day, a Friday, I worked in the cabin all day. The leg was stiff and I could barely walk. It rained all day but broke to clearing sun shortly before dusk.

I was supposed to keep my foot, my hurt leg, elevated, and so I lay upstairs on my bed reading and watching that autumn light on the aspen. At about six o'clock, I put the book down and dozed. Elizabeth and the girls were downstairs. I heard a tremendous baying — the sound the dogs make whenever a car comes down the long gravel driveway — but then I heard nothing else, and so I got up and went to the window. The pups were on their chains, looking up the driveway. Old Homer came walking stiff-legged down the drive, the way she does after a car or truck has left — after she has vanquished it.

I didn't see Colter. I figured he was down by my writing cabin. I went back and lay down. The doctor had said no hunting for ten to fourteen days, but I was hoping it would only have to be two or three.

An hour later, I knew somehow that he was gone. I could feel a huge absence, a strange emptiness. Alone, Colter never left the space between the house and the writing cabin. The pups would run rabbits whenever they got loose together, but never Colter.

I waited up all night that first night, and for many nights afterward. My knee healed quickly, and I scoured the woods with the other dogs for sign of a lion or wolf attack, but found nothing.

Earlier that afternoon, when Elizabeth and the girls had gotten back from town, I had lifted Lowry out of the truck, despite my knee, and carried her a short distance before setting her down to walk. Colter had come running up and had darted all around us, licking the heck out of her, like a puppy, and making her laugh. It was funny for a while, but then he kept licking her and wouldn't stop, and surely my last words to him, as I helped bring Lowry and the groceries inside, were something like, "Go on, now."

I remembered every hunt — every moment, every tree, every bush, the plucking of every bird. I remembered examining every crop, and what each bird had been eating.

A dog creates, transcribes, a new landscape for you.

A dog like Colter sharpens your joy of all the seasons, and for a while, sometimes a long while, such a dog seems capable, by himself alone, of holding time in place — of pinning it, and holding it taut. And then when he is gone, it is as if the world is taken away.

Dogs like that are young for what seems like a very long time.

On the second day of Colter's absence, I took Superman up the road. Hobbling on a cane, but carrying the gun, I was grieving already, as I watched Superman try to work the same woods Colter had raced through, knowing he could never, ever be the dog Colter was.

Just as I was thinking that — at that precise moment — I saw that Superman had gone on point, and that in front of him a young ruffed grouse was fanning. The late-day sun was shining on the bird and I knew then that someone, somewhere — perhaps Colter himself — was telling me Colter's hunt was over.

The bird flushed and I hit it, and Superman ran over to examine it, though again with a kind of professionalism — not the gonzo wild-eyed glee of Colter. I suspected Superman would be a perfect little grouse dog, but I realized now that that was not what I wanted — the cautiousness of a good grouse dog — though all along it is what I had believed I wanted.

Once you have lost a dog — especially the first you trained from a pup, the one you first set sail into the world with — you can never fully give of yourself to another dog. You can never again look at a dog you love without hedging a tiny bit, if only subconsciously, against the day when that dog, too, must leave. You can never again hunt or enter the future so recklessly, so joyously, without that weight of forethought.

Unlike Superman, Colter hadn't hunted so much to please me, in those first years, as to please the universe; and even as he began to mature, there was still always that feeling, that knowledge, that it was between the bird and him, and that I was merely fortunate enough to get to watch it.

Colter did not have to be "built up" in his training. Jarrett and I tried simply to bring in his borders and sharpen his focus, bit by bit, year by year, bird by bird. His joy, his fury to be in the field, was pure and irreducible. His two little brothers possess his talent but not his genius. They are only three years his ghosts, but it might as well be ten thousand years.

You never know when the last hunt is going to be. If you think about it at all, it is with the vague pleasure of distant daydreams, after thousands of hunts, not mere hundreds. You picture it at season's end, amidst snow and ice, and with the dog barely able to creep but still pushing resolutely forward, nearly blind and shivering but with his blood still as hot as when he was young.

Colter had his name and number on his collar. All I could figure was that someone drove down the driveway, perhaps mistaking it for a road, stopped, turned around when they saw our house, and that for some reason Colter followed that vehicle. Believing, perhaps, that that vehicle was going hunting. He'd never done such a thing before, but perhaps the vehicle had another dog, or dogs, in it. Maybe he was just desperate to go hunting.

I liked to imagine that he was still out there somewhere — perhaps a long way from Montana, hunting for someone else, or simply being a yard dog, sweet with children. I could not shake the hope that someday he would show up on the porch, ready to hunt again, or that I might get a phone call from someone saying, "I have a dog that sounds like he might be yours."

As I sleep restlessly, night after night, or more often, as I lie there awake, I can see him running and I feel guilty that I am not there to honor the birds he is finding; that I am not there to shoot them for him, as he keeps finding them. One way or the other, he is still out there running. He will never rest. There will always be this small gulf between us. I will always want him to know a moment's rest, and peace, and he will always know in his hot heart that the only peace to be gotten is by never resting, by always pushing on.

He is my Colter. Someone else may have fallen into possession of him — perhaps not knowing of his past — but when he runs, I am still his, and he is still mine.

Nineteen

In the rain, I took Point out into Colter's cover, a tiny little swamp pocket of aspen and cottonwoods, so dense with mulch and scent that even I could smell birds in there: a place so perfect for grouse that it seemed I could hear them scampering ahead of us across all those leaves. Rotting stumps, pools of water, mushrooms, frost-burned strawberry leaves, pearls of snowberries hanging ripe, autumn red globes of kinnickkinnick, and always, in Colter's cover, the near-hallucinogenic golds and yellows of the aspen and cottonwood, with their elegant white bark.

When I had first gotten Colter, Tim had taken me into this cover with his great dog Maddie. (Colter had still been too young to make the hunt.) Without meaning to insult the gods of the hunt, or grouse, I had foolishly proclaimed it the most beautiful cover I had ever seen, that the only thing missing from it was a liver-colored pointer, and I told Tim that I could already see brown Colter on point amidst this perfect yellow blaze of foliage. "Colter's Cover" we always called it, after that: and it was one of only two covers — two out of several dozen — where he never took a bird, and I accept the blame fully, for having mouthed off to the sky.

Point made game quickly, scurrying into the dense brush, and blew a bird out. Running through the upper part of the copse, he *was* beautiful, flashing young and square-headed through the autumn colors — and then I heard him yelping, caterwauling, as if he was being murdered with an ice pick, but the wails were racing into the distance seemingly at the speed of light, so that I knew he was following another flushed grouse to the horizon.

No yelling. I yelled myself out on Colter. After a while I traveled down into the cedar bottom to retrieve my lost dog and headed back to the truck, heart-whipped.

Walking out, going back through Colter's cover, we passed a scene of such breathtaking beauty that I had to pause and stare down at it, though it was with a strange and unfamiliar distancing, a disassociation from beauty observed. Amidst the black charcoal of an old burn crept the bright frost-red leaves of wild strawberry plants, tangled up with the rain-wet yellow leaves of cottonwoods. It had finally gotten here, as it always did: autumn. Without Colter, though, the beauty was only skin-deep, and I realized how addicted I had become to him, and his talent, his burning heart. I could still recognize the beauty, but there was that kick missing to it, an electricity. I was not wired to Colter anymore, nor he to me, and I had never realized so fully — or rather, so consciously, so analytically — how much the beauty of these woods depended on him.

I stared at the beautiful colors on the surface — red, yellow, char-black — and breathed the autumn scents, but I could not dig deeper, by myself. It was simply and only beautiful — nothing more. I called to Point and we went on home.

Twenty

I CONTINUED, to the obvious dismay of family and friends, to hold on to that most expensive, extravagant of emotions: hope. I continued to place ads in the newspapers and hunting and fishing magazines, all through the fall and across the winter and into the next spring: trying hard to summon him to me, and imagining, at indulgent moments of the day, and in the early evenings, that this was all only a phase, a test — a strange period through which we would both pass, and that when we were reunited, by one miracle or another, the hunts would be sweeter. I sketched pictures of him returning to me, bounding across a field, joyous.

It was May sixteenth — a green, lovely day, with the promise of the new life of the year only recently emerging from the snow, when Joanne, Tim's wife, called me from the pay phone at the mercantile. She had heard a mushroom hunter say he had found the skeleton of a dog back in the woods a couple of miles from my house, off to the side of a logging road: a big dog. She handed the phone to the man, and he asked me if the dog had been wearing a red collar.

I don't remember the shape and size and particular feel of the sorrow when I found him. I remember that it was a warm day and that I sat slumped with him in the shade of a big cedar tree. I remember the beautiful shape of his big bright skull, and the amazing teeth, all revealed now. The vacant eye sockets — *my Colter* — with which we had both seen so much.

There was a bullet hole through his spine — .22 caliber. Had he been running? Standing broadside? Approaching the shooter with a friendly grin? Did he die instantly, or scrabbling in the leaves? Sitting there under the cedar tree, stunned and crying, and in the weeks that followed, and still today, I had to ask the question *Why?*

I gathered all the parts. His dog tags jingled and his bones rang with a dull light clatter as I placed him in the back of the truck. I felt something emptier than loneliness on the drive home.

I buried him next to my cabin door, in that sunken, blissful spot where he had napped, always waiting for the next hunt: beneath the wild rose bushes. I buried him, as I had Ann, with bones and antlers and venison and dog food and a wreath of cedar and lupine. I buried him with shells, both 12- and 20-gauge, for whenever we went hunting again, and I put in extras because I knew I'd miss some shots. The bones and wings of his quarry. A whistle, a brass bell. Then the earth back in over him, and new grief in over old grief, like a mountain eroding to bury with its disintegrating sediments, disintegrating heart and body, something bright and valuable below.

Epilogue

A MONTH LATER, an animal shelter over in Idaho
called. They had heard we had been looking for our
big brown male German shorthair, and they had one.
They knew it wasn't Colter (it didn't have his pet ID
chip), but they wanted to know if we might be interested in adopting him. He was a sweet dog, they said,
but had been there a week, and was scheduled to be
put down the next day.

I had my hands more than full with Point and
Superman, as well as old blind Homer, but Elizabeth
drove over to look at the dog.

When she got home that evening she told me he
was calm and friendly but big — huge — and that he
minded really well, which raised my suspicions that
he might not be pure German shorthair, but some kind
of mix. He drooled a good bit, and his eyes were red
and crusty with some infection picked up on the road,
and he tried to hump any other dog he got near, but all

in all he seemed like a fine dog. Whenever a bird flew over the dog would stop what he was doing and stare up at it, perfectly frozen, and lift his paw.

According to the policy of the animal shelter, the price of this dog's bail was neutering. They said they had located his old owner, who had told them his name was Indy and that if anyone wanted him, they could have him.

If someone picked up Colter, and he'd ended up in the same fix, we would have liked to believe that someone would have posted his bail, if that's what it took to keep him alive.

I first saw him on the day of the nut-cutting. A lady from the clinic took us out back — past the yowling kittens and yapping terriers, a deafening montage of testimony to our careless, reckless need for companionship, friendship, even love, regardless of the consequences — and stretched out in the back kennel, a deadweight, was a huge gaunt brown dog, with a head like a bull. Pus was leaking from his pink eyes, a trail of drool issued from his mouth, and he was quivering at the din, every muscle twitching and shuddering involuntarily. He looked up at me, drugged — trying to lift his head to evaluate me, but unable to. I crouched beside him and touched his ribs. *So this is what it comes to*, I thought, remembering Colter — remembering his grace and speed and power. *This is the trade you make*, I thought, studying the quivering dog, who looked to be at least ten years old.

I sat there for a long time, remembering Colter, before finally finding a thought in my mind that made any kind of sense, and the thought was: *Well, anyway, he doesn't deserve to die.*

We went back and picked him up the next day, and he looked immensely better: I'd never seen such resiliency. When we got home, he *glided* out of the truck, moving with an eerie, effortless motion that was made all the more striking and odd by his hugeness. You could see the ghost of power and grace within him. Anyone could see it.

High-stepping like a show horse, he examined the house. He stopped and lifted his paw in a point and gazed soulfully at the sky when a raven flew past — and long after the raven was gone he remained on point, staring into the curious distance, as if somehow traveling, in his mind at least, with that gone-away bird.

After he understood that the bird wasn't coming back, Indy eased gracefully out of his point, and, as if to prove himself the perfect bird dog, he went over and picked up a stick and brought it back to me to play fetch: a retriever as well as a pointer.

He leaned against my thigh, huge and mellow, and I had the troubling thought that if he ran into me in the field, he could knock me over.

I tossed his stick for him several more times. Even when he wasn't playing fetch, he carried sticks and other objects around in his mouth, including a stump nearly as big as a car tire, his neck muscles straining, as if to prove that, though technically a perfect dog — points, retrieves, etc. — he had in him also an element of that goofiness that I so admire in a bird dog, and which the best pointers seem to have in spades. It was like some secret Masonic handshake, that revelation of goofiness: him carrying the stump around like that.

When I introduced him to old blind Homer, she merely sniffed him briefly, then accepted him as she had always, eventually, accepted all of my eccentricities, this nutless giant being merely another in a long list of changes she's had to adapt to over the course of her long life. Little Point-Man's eyes got huge, however, and he raised his hackles and skittered away (Superman was down in Texas, being trained by Jarrett). Indy gave short, furious chase, they growled ferociously, Indy gently mouthed Point's little neck and then that was that: Indy agreed not to break Point's neck, and Point agreed not to growl again.

The dogs all slept together like a pack, that night, and I pondered the hunting season that was not so distant. I wondered what kind of grouse dog that nifty-footed, obedient, trotting-horse dog might make, and what it might be like to see him coming back with a big pheasant or even — greedy, greedy — a duck or a goose in his mouth.

I wasn't happy, and wasn't over Colter, not by a long shot, nor will I ever be — but I could feel things turning in my heart, old muscles, and echoes that I had not felt or heard in a long time, as I began to consider, and hope. I decided to go ahead and dream. He wasn't Colter, but I let myself believe that Colter had sent him.

The next day we had a barbecue at the house. My friend Jesse was logging with his big draft horses,

Buster and Brown, on our property across the road, and Jesse and his sawyer and the sawyer's son came over, as did a few other friends. We were grilling venison burgers and sitting around in the cooling twilight in that incredible mid-June forever-evening sun-struck green light — the fields and meadows and forest glowing, passing the sunlight through each thin new green blade of grass, each new leaf; and Indy, the newcomer, was trotting around in the yard, shining like rich chocolate in that sunlight. The children were playing with him, chasing him in circles (he tolerated them, stayed always ahead of them in his high-footed, steady canter), from time to time he would stop and stare upwards at birds passing overhead. All in all it was simply one of those perfect summer evenings whose majesty is strangely in no way diminished by your heightened awareness of the moment's perfection, and of its brevity, and I could feel some percolation or fizz in my blood that made my heart beat stronger and my eyes shine brighter. Something opened my imagination back into greater terrain.

We tend — despite our best protestations — not to want a happy ending. Some strange part of us wants, as story listeners, scars across the heart, and the stratification of that tissue: lithification, rigidity, character tested by hardship. The dignity of mortal endurance; a graceless, clumsy, *human* aging, and an excess of rot, in the aftermath of a story of childish luck and innocence. Stories containing too much bounty seem always too, well, *childish*.

Early the next morning, as I walked Indy and Point-

Man, Indy galloped over to Point, nipped him on the flank, and they set off down the road yipping and howling. I yelled, afraid that Indy was following some vague heart's-pull back to Idaho — and that he was taking Point-Man with him. Soon the yipping faded away, and they were gone. I wondered if Indy was an incarnation of Cerberus, the great-headed dog from the underworld, come to teach me the ancient lesson reserved for most fools: *Stop whining, look around, and be grateful for what you've still got.* I had had so much in the way of dogs, and now I had only an old blind hound, Homer. From riches to rags, with bird season only a handful of weeks away. I blushed at the name of my sin, *gluttony*.

Again, I did everything you have to do: ran radio and newspaper ads all across the Northwest, drove or hiked to the tops of mountains, and looked and listened. I plotted various routes back toward Idaho and traveled them, searching for sign: for tracks, for spoor. I visited neighbors, put up posters: when people assured me that dogs always came home, I explained the dilemma that Indy probably wouldn't be coming home because he had no home to come to.

Over the course of a week, a few reports drifted in. A woman over in Idaho, fifty miles distant, had seen a little spotted dog, a shorthair, running hard down a dirt road. Back in Montana, some people outside a bar named the Red Dog had seen a big reddish-brown friendly shorthair that sounded like Indy, forty miles in the other direction; but he had vanished when I went to look for him.

More sleepless days and nights passed — waking often to the imagined or hoped-for sounds of the dogs on the front porch, coming to the bowls of food I had left for them — and gradually, agonizingly, I began to consider letting go of hope.

On the afternoon of the seventh day, a neighbor who lived a mile up the road came driving up with a gaunt-ribbed, shred-footed Indy. His eyes and lips were scratched from what must have been headlong passage through miles of brush. He had violent diarrhea, an insatiable appetite, and I was glad to see him, very glad, but the barb of sorrow sank deeper as I realized that I'd effectively traded my great young dog, Colter's brother, for this huge unknown creature. I knew I was staring at a lesson, but couldn't quite think of what it might be.

That night, the same neighbor came driving up with the thoroughly emaciated little Point-Man, who, despite his extreme exhaustion, nonetheless went into his usual gymnastics (tail-rotoring, dancing, yipping) at the sight of me.

I set about building a fence the next day, determined to try to hold on to, and be grateful for, what I've still got, as well as for that which I continue to receive.

Colter was probably the greatest pointer who ever ran. There will always be a hollow spot in me, a burnt circle in the bottom of my stomach, whenever I think of him: as if I am carrying a bucket of hot, hot ashes in the bottom of my stomach — the memory of how he ran, the memory of how he was.

Things will never be the same. I have a young brown skulking dog training down in Texas, however, and a sneaky little creeping pointed dog, and a new strange big brown dog who still continues to stop at the strangest times and freeze and stare up at the sky so intently as to perhaps cause even time to pause for a moment — for just a moment — to admire all the beauty below, including that big muscular brown dog on point, before moving on.

It's the strangest thing. Even after burying his bones, I have the feeling, every day, that I'm going to see him again — am going to hunt with him again, at least once more.

ACKNOWLEDGMENTS

PORTIONS OF THIS BOOK first appeared, in different form, in *Sports Afield, Five Points, Ascent, Oxford American, The Bark, Texas, Southern Review, Shooting Sportsman,* and *Pointing Dog Journal;* I am grateful to the editors of these magazines. Friends and hunting partners who spent time with Colter and me in the field, and for whom I'll always be grateful, include my wife, Elizabeth, and our daughters, Mary Katherine and Lowry; Colter's "parents," Tom Oar and Nancy Weaver; my hunting partners, Tim Linehan and Maddie, Todd Tanner, Jim Fergus, Doug Tate, and Tim Crawford; my father, C. R. Bass; Colter's trainer, Jarrett Thompson; my typist, Angi Young; my agent, Bob Dattila; Colter's vet, Doug Griffiths; and my editors, Harry Foster, Dorothy Henderson, and Camille Hykes. And thanks to Elizabeth Hughes Bass for further editorial assistance.

In his masterpiece, *A Hunter's Road,* Jim Fergus eloquently addresses a concern I share regarding writing about and celebrating what is essentially a solitary endeavor. The last thing I'd want to be a party to, in extolling the wonders

187

of a dog like Colter — so superior a representative of his breed — would be to encourage readers to go out and purchase German shorthair pups, or any other hunting breed, and then not hunt them. I'm extremely fortunate to be able to hunt one hundred days a year, if I wish, and I recognize fully the rarity of this good fortune.

Fergus writes: "It is not the author's intention to serve as chamber of commerce, to promote the sport of hunting, or to advise the reader where, or with whom, to go bird hunting; there are plenty of organizations, publications and individuals already in that business."

To be more blunt: unlike the sports of, say, fly fishing and downhill skiing, bird hunting is, however regrettable this may be, not a pursuit for one or two weekends a year or for the odd vacation. I believe a hunting dog, bred by man and time and landscape and quarry for only one burning purpose, deserves to be hunted steadfastly if not tirelessly, or not at all. I would be remiss if I failed to stress this conviction — again, while marveling at my good fortune in having been able to give my dog Colter the thing he was born for: a seemingly endless run of days in the field and in the wild forests.

To take such a spirited breed, such a spirited dog, and give him or her anything less would be, to my way of thinking, a sad and serious thing indeed.

WHERE THE SEA USED TO BE

The first full-length novel by one of our finest fiction writers, *Where the Sea Used to Be* tells the story of a struggle between a father and his daughter for the souls of two men, Mathew and Wallis — his protégés, her lovers.   ISBN 0-395-95781-8, $14.00

THE SKY, THE STARS, THE WILDERNESS

Here is Bass at his magical, passionate, and lyrical best. In three novellas, a woman returns to live on her family's Texas ranch, a man tracks his wife through a winter wilderness, and an ancient ocean buried in the foothills of the Appalachians becomes a battleground for a young wildcat oilman and his aging mentor.

ISBN 0-395-92475-8, $12.00

THE BOOK OF YAAK

The Yaak Valley of northwestern Montana is one of the last great wild places in the United States. Bass captures the soul of the Yaak Valley and reveals how, if places like Yaak are lost, so too will be the human riches of mystery and imagination.

ISBN 0-395-87746-6, $12.00

THE LOST GRIZZLIES
A Search for Survivors in the Wilderness of Colorado

Bass turns his considerable talents to an evocation of wilderness beauty and the history of human encroachment that may, or may not, have wiped out the last of these massive, solitary bears from their southern range.   ISBN 0-395-85700-7, $13.00

IN THE LOYAL MOUNTAINS

In these dazzling short stories only Rick Bass could write, enormous pigs charge through the streets and root under houses, a woman runs up and down mountains, and a group of children in wolf masks chase a boy through the woods.   ISBN 0-395-87747-4, $12.00

WINTER
Notes from Montana

In a celebration of winter in the last valley of Montana without electricity, Bass describes the wildness and freedom of valley people, the slow-motion quality of life, and the dangers of the wilderness.

ISBN 0-395-61150-4, $12.00